# The K98k Rifle

©Copyright 2002
Second, revised edition, ©2010


The K98k Rifle
The Propaganda Photo Series, Volume I
by G. de Vries & B.J. Martens


ISBN 978-90-805583-1-1


Published by
**S.I. Publicaties BV**
**P.O. Box  188**
**6860 AD Oosterbeek**
**The Netherlands**

**Fax: (+)31-26-4430824**
**E-mail: si@sipublicaties.nl**
**Website: www.sipublicaties.nl**


Design & lay-out by Grafisch Bureau Bekkers, Soest,
The Netherlands
Printed in the Netherlands

# CONTENTS

(Museum of Modern History, Slovenia, No. 6605/13).

# PREFACE

## The *Propaganda* series

The *Propaganda* series is a new series of books on World War II German small arms. Each volume covers all essential information on history and development, ammunition and accessories, codes and markings and contains photos of nearly every model and accessory.

The most important quality of the *Propaganda* series however, is a unique selection of original German World War II propaganda photos. The combination of solid information and original photos makes the *Propaganda* series the most extensive and reliable source of German small arms 'in-use', depicting weapons and their accessories as they were actually used.

The propaganda photos were collected from German and other archives, and were taken by official German war photographers. During World War II, there were about 2,500 official photographers and reporters, usually organized in special propaganda units covering all branches of the armed forces on all fronts. Their work was considered so important, that some of them were given permits that gave them immediate access to any form of transport at any time on any front.

The photographs were used by the Nazipress in Germany and the occupied countries to persuade the population of the Third Reich 'point of view', as directed by the Ministry of Propaganda. Therefore, most of the original captions are very misleading or even flagrant lies, while the majority of the photos are posed. Some photos were found to be retouched to conceal the exact location or to add a Nazi-symbol. Keeping these restrictions in the back of one's mind, the photos nevertheless offer the most adequate information on the small arms as they were actually used.

For this purpose they are published in a large format and separately from the text. The photos are classified into groups, depicting various aspects of the K98k: training and education; cleaning and repair; special equipment and accessoires; sniping and K98k variations; and general pictures of the K98k in use.

## ACKNOWLEDGEMENTS

This book could not have been published without the assistance of the following institutions and individuals:
- Bundesamt für Wehrtechnik und Beschaffung, Wehrtechnische Studiensammlung (WTS), Koblenz, Germany: Dr. R. Wirtgen, Mr. H. Heinrich, Mr. W. Oster
- Bundesarchiv Koblenz, Germany: Mrs. B. Kuhl
- Mr. D.J. Hueting, Renkum, The Netherlands
- Ministry of Defence Pattern Room, Nottingham, United Kingdom: Mr. H Woodend, Mr. R. Jones, Mr. J. Henshaw, Mr. N. Dixon, Mr. E. Rose, Mr. R. Sharrock, Mrs. C. Groves
- Musée d'Armes, Liège, Belgium: Dr. C. Gaier
- Museum of Modern History, Ljubljana, Slovenia: Dr. D. Voncina, Mr. V. Martincic, Mrs. M. Kokalj Kocevar
- Mr. H.L. Visser, Wassenaar, The Netherlands

## PHOTO CREDITS

The pictures in this book were acquired from the following collections:
- Bundesamt für Wehrtechnik und Beschaffung, Wehrtechnische Studiensammlung, Koblenz, Germany (WTS, Koblenz)
- Ministry of Defence Pattern Room, Nottingham, United Kingdom (MoD Pattern Room, Nottingham)
- Bundesarchiv, Koblenz, Germany
- Museum of Modern History, Ljubljana, Slovenia
- Süddeutsche Zeitung, Münich, Germany

# INTRODUCTION

## The K98k

The *Karabiner 98 kurz* (Carbine 98, short) was the main small arm of the German armed forces during World War II. It was used by all branches of the army from 1935 until the very last days of the Third Reich in early May, 1945. The weapon was officially designated 'carbine', but with its 60 cm barrel and 111 cm overall length the K98k was actually a rifle, as it is referred to in this book. 'Carbine' was a tactical designation, meaning the weapon featured side mounted slings and a bent-down bolt handle, to facilitate transport and handling by the cavalry and other specialized branches, for which carbines were originally intended.

Although the mechanism was developed in the 19th century, the K98k was among the best bolt action weapons of World War II and it fired a powerful cartridge. The quality of the Mauser 98 mechanism is illustrated by the late-war production K98k's, which were simplified and of very crude finish, but still featured the reliability and accuracy of the pre-war production weapons.

In the course of the war, however, the German army encountered a growing number of enemy soldiers equipped with semi-automatic rifles: Russian Simonovs and Tokarevs at first, later also the American Garand. Notwithstanding its qualities, the K98k remained a bolt action rifle, more tiring to operate and with a lower rate of fire. Nevertheless, despite much development work and the adoption of the G41 and G43 semi-automatic rifles and the Sturmgewehr, the K98k remained by far the most important German battle rifle.

From its adoption in June, 1935, until early 1945, about 12 million K98k's were made. The firm of Mauser was predominant, but there were nine other manufacturers. For reasons of rationalization, the design and production process were gradually simplified. But the demands for K98k's were never met, especially because of heavy losses: before the end of the war, two-thirds of all K98k's were reported lost. Therefore, simultaneously with the K98k, the German army used many older converted system 98 weapons and a great quantity of captured foreign rifles, some very similar to the K98k.

# I EARLY DEVELOPMENTS

## The Gewehr 98, the K98 and the K98a

The standard small arm of the German infantry during World War I was the *Gewehr 98*. This was Paul Mauser's (1838-1914) last major bolt action design. The *Gewehr 98* was a strong and reliable rifle, featuring a 74 cm barrel with an overall length of 125 cm. The cavalry and other branches were armed with the *Karabiner 98(a)*, which was adopted in 1908. This weapon had a forerunner, designated *Karabiner 98*, the first of all 'system 98' carbines.

Development of the *Karabiner 98* began in the late 1890's. Troop tests with cavalry and artillery carbines were held in 1899, and in 1902 a model was approved as the 'Karabiner 98'. The *Karabiner 98*, or Carbine 98, featured the *Gewehr 98* bolt mechanism, a 43.5 cm barrel (overall length 96 cm), and a bent-down bolt handle(1).

Only three years after the official adoption of this weapon, the military faced an unpleasant surprise. While the carbine was designed for the 88 cartridge, the new, more powerful 'S' cartridge (*Spitzgeschoss*: pointed bullet) was adopted. Both the rifle and carbine 98 had to be modified, by reaming out the chamber and adapting the sights to the new ammunition. The 43.5 cm barrel, however, proved too short and the carbine produced a very loud blast and an impressive muzzle flash.

This was unpleasant for the shooter's neighbors, but also made the marksman easy to trace, especially at night. The only solution was to develop a longer-barreled type and thus the production of the original Carbine 98 was halted by early 1905.

The Rifle Testing Commission in Spandau immediately started designing a new model. This became the Carbine 98AZ (*Aufpflanz- und Zusammensetzvorrichtung*: bayonet-attachment and stacking hook), later renamed to Carbine 98 and in 1923 finally to Carbine 98a. It differed from the first model Carbine 98 in having a 59 cm barrel (overall length 109 cm), a new type of sliding sight, a lengthened handguard and a round, bent-down bolt handle with a cut-out stock.

The Carbine 98a was approved by the German Kaiser in January 1908 and first handed out to troops in 1909. It became the standard small arm of machine gun units, foot artillery, technical and supply units and the cavalry. About 1.5 million carbines of this type were produced between 1908 and 1918.

During the First World War, the German army was confronted with serious shortcomings of both the 98 rifle and carbine. The first proved to be too long for trench warfare and featured a backsight graduation in 100m increments from 400 to 2000 meters, while many targets were engaged at a shorter distance. The barrel of the carbine, on the other hand, appeared to be too short. It still produced such a strong muzzle flash, that first-line elite troops, armed with carbines, were provided with auxiliary barrel extensions. Moreover, manufacture of both a rifle and a carbine model seriously slowed down production.

## The Bicyclist's rifle and the K98b

Besides from the *Gewehr 98* and the *Karabiner K98a*, there was a third World War I Mauser 98 model. This was the so-called *Radfahrer Gewehr* (Bicyclist's rifle), manufactured in limited amounts before the war to

The Gewehr 98 was the standard small arm of the German army in World War I. The letters 'E.W.B.' on the butt stand for *Einwohnerwehr Bayern* (Residents defense force, Bavaria) and were added in 1919 or 1920 (# 8847n, WTS Koblenz).

The Carbine 98 was the first of all 'system 98' carbines. This specimen was manufactured in Erfurt in 1905 (# 0147, WTS Koblenz).

The K98a was adopted in 1908 and was the standard carbine of the cavalry and other branches during W.W.I. Note the stacking hook and the front sight protectors (# 814, WTS Koblenz).

arm bicycle troops. The *Radfahrer Gewehr* featured the same length and weight as the rifle. It only differed in a sidemounted sling, a curved bolt handle with finger recess underneath and a widened lower band. Although the Bicycle units were soon dissolved and incorporated into the infantry, the Bicyclist's rifle was not forgotten*(2)*.

The Treaty of Versailles of 1919 limited the German army to 100,000 men and exactly defined the amount and types of weapons. The *Reichswehr*, as the new army was called, was allowed 84,000 rifles and 18,000 carbines of the 98 type (later on, 25% extra for reserve). Thus the *Reichswehr* was initially armed with carbines 98(a) in their original form and World War I rifles, which from about 1922 onward got new sights.

However, the *Reichswehr* soon started a search for a universal weapon to replace both existing types. The Bicyclist's rifle became the focus of attention. This model seemed particularly suited for the new, universal concept; it had the same ballistic performance as the rifle, but due to the sidemounted sling and curved bolt handle it was more comfortable to carry. Moreover, this model was easy to manufacture, either by converting existing rifles, or by small changes to the production line of the *Gewehr 98*.

In 1923, the former *Radfahrer Gewehr*, provided with a new tangent sight and a bolt stop acting on an empty magazine, was adopted as the *Karabiner 98b*.

The K98b was initially manufactured by converting rifles. From 1926 onward, it was also newly made by Simson & Co in Suhl, allowed by the Versailles Treaty as the only arms manufacturer for the German army. It is believed that about 25,000 K98b's were produced*(3)*. Although the *Reichswehr* had the intention to make it the standard arm of all branches, this plan was never executed. Money was short, production slow, and soon there were complaints about its length - again.

## Commercial short rifles

While the German military was trying to solve its rifle problem, several private companies had started manufacturing a modernized Mauser carbine. In the early twenties, both FN of Herstal, Belgium and the Czech state arms factory of Brno (which had acquired the Mauser W.W.I *Gewehr 98* production line) had developed a modernized, shortened rifle with a 60 cm barrel and a 98 mechanism, designated Model 24 and Vz24 respectively. These weapons were an immediate commercial success and exported to many countries.

So in 1924, German soldiers were complaining about their long rifles and carbines, while two foreign companies were making good profits with modern, short Mauser rifles. This was a situation which could not last for long, and it didn't.

Somewhere in the mid-twenties, Mauser decided to enter the military market again with a new rifle. This became the first type Mauser *Standard Modell*. It was very similar to the Czech and Belgian Model 1924 short rifles. It had a barrel of 60 cm and a redesigned rearsight, a straight bolt handle, bottom sling swivels and finger grooves in the stock.

Since German companies were still not allowed to manufacture military weapons, many of the *Standard Modell* short rifles were sold via Switzerland. Mauser had acquired a company in the Swiss town of Kreuzlingen were the Oberndorf-manufactured rifle parts were assembled, tested and finally shipped to their customers. The *Standard Modell* was sold to many foreign armies, but to some local customers as well: the

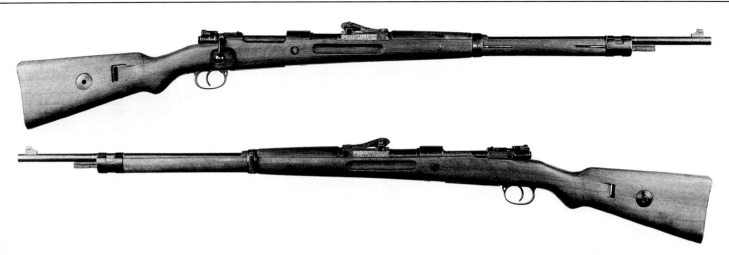

The Bicyclist's Rifle or *Radfahrer Gewehr* was used in early W.W.I on a very limited scale. Apart from the bent-down bolt handle and the side-mounted sling it was identical to the *Gewehr 98* (# 2741, WTS Koblenz).

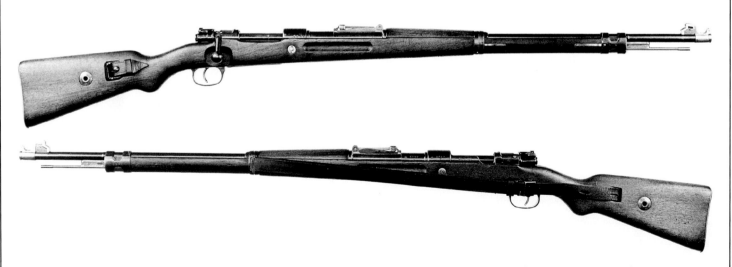

The K98b. Externally, the only difference between the K98b and the Bicyclist's Rifle was the new tangent sight. In 1929/1930 shortened K98b's were tested alongside the *Standard Modell I* (# 3869, WTS Koblenz).

newly formed SA (*Sturm Abteilung*) and SS (*Schutz Staffel*) from Hitler's Nazi party.

Hitler became *Reichschancellor* one day before the second International Disarmament Conference opened, on January 31, 1933. He immediately left the conference, when France insisted on demands against German rearmament. Soon afterward, Hitler withdrew Germany from the League of Nations. Only a few months later he introduced a secret rearmament programm and allotted an enormous amount of money for this purpose. The main problem of the Army, the lack of funds, was now solved and the long search for a new standard rifle would soon come to an end.

## Mauser Standard Model II: the pre-adoption K98k

Although detailed information is missing, there is no doubt that Mauser and the military worked together closely in developing the new, universal rifle. The story began in about 1923, when the military voiced its thoughts about a universal rifle. Some two years later, Mauser introduced the first version of the *Standard Modell*, featuring a 60 cm barrel. The designation 'Standard' was not chosen by coincidence, but referred to the universal or standard rifle the *Reichswehr* was looking for.

The K98b, as mentioned before, was initially intended for that purpose, but it proved to be too long. In 1929, technical experiments and troop trials were held with shortened K98b's, featuring 67 cm and 60 cm barrels with a bent-down bolt handle and side-mounted sling swivels. The shortened K98b was subsequently tested alongside the Mauser *Standard Modell* in early 1930.

The military preferred the short-barreled K98b over the commercial Mauser, since it was more comfortable to handle due to its curved bolt handle and side-mounted sling swivels. Again it was considered to adopt this weapon as the universal rifle, but even shortening and converting all existing *Gewehr 98's* and *Karabiner 98b's* to the new configuration in a short time span was too expensive. It was therefore decided to gradually shorten these weapons from about 1932 onward(4).

Hitler's introduction of the secret rearmament program, however, speeded things up. By late 1933, early 1934 an improved version of the *Standard Modell* was introduced, featuring a bent-down bolt handle and side-mounted sling swivels. This *Standard Modell II* was thus the pre-adoption K98k. Apart from the grasping grooves and the absence of a bolt-stop and bolt disassembly disc, it was completely similar to the 1934 Sauer & Sohn manufactured K98k's. These weapons, in turn, only differed from the standard, early-war production K98k in having two band springs instead of one, to retain both the upper and the lower band.

Most of the *Standard Modell II* rifles feature stock markings as 'D.R.P.' (*Deutsche Reichspost*: postal service), 'D.R.' (*Deutsche Reichsbahn*: railway service) and 'Ch.d.A.' (*Chef des Amtes*: chief of an unspecified institution). It is reported the designation D.R.P. was a sort of code name for short rifles which were delivered to the SA, SS and other Nazi-organizations. Some researchers consider this weapon to be the immediate predecessor of the K98k(5). Although many of these weapons were actually acquired by several Nazi-organizations, the D.R.P. rifle was a mere variant of the second version of the *Standard Modell*.

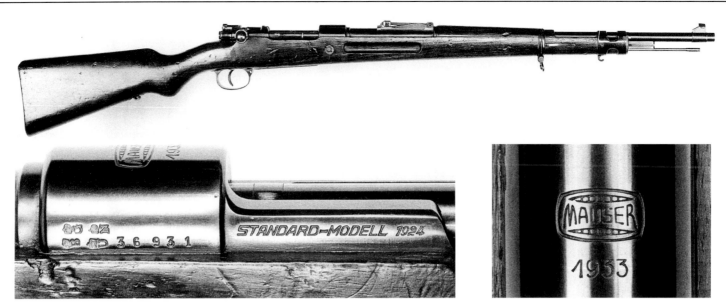

The *Standard Modell I* was introduced in the mid-twenties. After the comparative trials with the shortened K98b, it was succeeded by an improved version with a curved bolt handle (# 36931, WTS Koblenz).

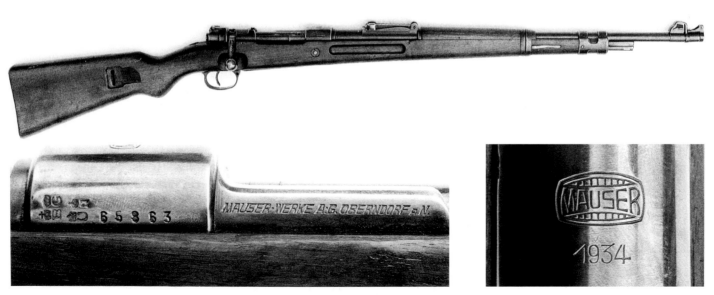

This *Standard Modell II* was the pre-adoption K98k. Apart from the grasping grooves in the handguard and the absence of the bolt disassembly disc and the bolt stop, this rifle is the same as the 1934 Sauer & Sohn manufactured K98k's. This specimen is marked *D.R.P.* on the left side of the butt (# 65863, H.L. Visser).

# II  THE K98k

## The K98k is adopted

The official army journal of the war ministry, the *Allgemeine Heeresmitteilungen* of June 21, 1935, officially announced the adoption of the K98k on June 14, 1935. Initially, its code name was *Adalbert*; in 1944 this was changed to *Dauerwelle*. Already in mid-1934, first Mauser and then Sauer & Sohn had started production. The *Karabiner 98 kurz* was thus already manufactured before the offical date of adoption. This indicates the decision to adopt the weapon was made early in 1934.

With the adoption of the K98k, the World War II German army was equipped with a carbine with nearly the same dimensions and characteristics as during the First World War. But despite the small external differences, the K98k had a far better performance; while the W.W.I K98a fired the 'S cartridge', the K98k used the 'sS cartridge', the *schweres Spitzgeschoss* or heavy ball.

Another major difference was the concept of the 'universal rifle'. Since there was one model for all branches of the armed forces, the production process was easier and faster then in World War I, when both a rifle and a carbine were manufactured. As described below, production figures were (and still are) an important and much discussed subject.

## Production figures

Probably the most discussed aspect of the K98k is how many of these weapons were actually produced. In this respect, only one thing is certain: this problem will never be solved. Many manufacturers archives are lost. Army inventory lists were inconsequential in distinguishing 'original' K98k's from foreign, but very

similar, weapons. Converted rifles and K98b's were often listed as 'original' K98k's, but probably did not figure in the records of newly produced weapons. An unknown quantity of rifles were reconditioned and subsequently reissued, further spoiling the statistics. And finally, production figures were for propaganda purposes as well, and are therefore often misleading.

Keeping these restrictions in the back of one's mind, an approximate reconstruction is nevertheless possible. This is due to the detailed research of some authors, and the fact that some reliable figures are known. In this respect, the books of R.D. Law, H.D. Handrich and A. Wacker (see chapter IX) offer the most detailed information.

The first list (Estimated K98k production) is a rational adaption of these author's figures. It includes newly produced K98k's, converted K98b's and Gewehr 98's, as well as 'foreign' K98k-type rifles, like the Polish Wz29/40.

To illustrate the problems involved in tracing the most reliable figures, a second list is published. It features the figures from a monthly, secret overview, titled 'Survey of required and accepted amount of small arms' (*Geheime Kommandosache. Überblick über den Rüstungsstand von Waffen, Wa J Rü [Wu G 2]*). According to this second list, approximately 1.8 million K98k's were manufactured and accepted by the Army in 1943. Since the Army usually acquired around 90% of total production, the actual amount manufactured in 1943 was approximately 2 million. Compared to the first list, there is a difference of about 370,000 weapons.

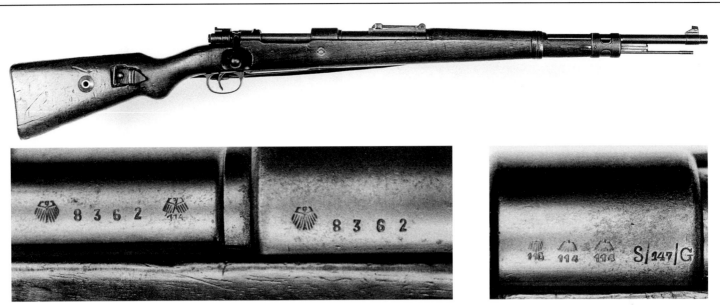

A K98k made by Sauer & Sohn in 1935 before the official adoption. Unlike rifles produced later, the manufacturer's code (S/147/G) is on the right side of the receiver ring. Also note the Weimar-eagle proof and the Weimar-eagle/114 Waffenamt (# 8362, MoD Pattern Room, Nottingham).

A *Gewehr 98* converted to K98k specifications. Unlike most Gewehr 98/K98k conversions, this rifle was fitted with a new, laminated stock. Note the Nazi-eagle firing proof (*Beschussstempel*) left of the serial number (# XX8566, MoD Pattern Room, Nottingham).

| Estimated K98k production | | Newly produced & accepted K98k's, 1943 | |
|---|---|---|---|
| 1934 | 23,000 | January | 82,017 |
| 1935 | 270,000 | February | 113,426 |
| 1936 | 525,000 | March | 137,191 |
| 1937 | 685,000 | April | 150,880 |
| 1938 | 911,000 | May | 154,924 |
| 1939 | 1,036,000 | June | 152,200 |
| 1940 | 1,329,000 | July | 164,471 |
| 1941 | 1,287,000 | August | 154,200 |
| 1942 | 1,245,000 | September | 172,106 |
| 1943 | 2,373,000 | Oktober | 176,200 |
| 1944 | 2,081,000 | November | 165,900 |
| 1945 | 235,000 | December | 170,709 |
| Total | 12,000,000 | Total | 1,794,224 |

## Manufacturers

The K98k was first manufactured by Mauser and Sauer & Sohn. After the government acquired a license from Mauser, these companies were followed by Erma (later renamed Feinmechanische Werke), the Berlin-Lübecker Maschinenfabrik, Berlin-Suhler-Waffen und Fahrzeugwerke, Gustloff Werke, Steyr-Daimler-Puch and two companies in the occupied Czechoslavakian town of Brno: Waffen Werke Brünn & Waffen Werke Bystrica.

Contrary to popular belief, there was no practice of simply adding more manufacturers to increase production. As the following list shows, the Berlin-Suhler-Waffen und Fahrzeugwerke, Erma/Feinmechanische Werke and the Berlin-Lübecker Maschinenfabrik halted production in the first half of the war.

This was due to the rationalization of the German war industry, from late 1941 onward. The purpose of these politics was the saving of raw materials, time, and labor forces, and to achieve the highest possible production figures. Therefore, many companies received orders to halt manufacture of a certain product and to concentrate all efforts on the production of other war material.

## Design changes

To keep up with demand and to save material, workforce and time, the K98k design and production process was simplified again and again. However, the first changes in 1939 concerned improvements. The cleaning rod was lengthened from 25 to 32 cm, so that the rod holding bearing could be placed deeper into the stronger middle stock, to prevent cracking the front part of the stock. A sight hood was adopted to protect the front sight, together with a rubber muzzle cap. Apart from these changes, all other modifications were intended to save time, money and material.

From about 1939 onward, the walnut stocks were replaced by laminated stocks and the milled flat butt plates were replaced by pressed sheet-metal caps that enclosed the butt end. Pressed sheet-metal parts

## Manufacturers, time period and estimated K98k production

| | | | |
|---|---|---|---|
| Mauser, Oberndorf | 1934 - 1945 | 4,400,000 | (36,7%) |
| Mauser, Borsigwalde | 1935 - 1944 | 933,000 | (7,8%) |
| Sauer & Sohn, Suhl | 1934 - 1944 | 1,700,000 | (14,1%) |
| Erma/Feinmechanische Werke, Erfurt | 1935 - 1941 | 562,000 | (4,7%) |
| Berlin-Lübecker Maschinenfabrik, Lübeck | 1936 - 1942 | 754,000 | (6,3%) |
| Berlin-Suhler-Waffen und Fahrzeugwerke | 1937 - 1939 | 132,000 | (1,1%) |
| Gustloff Werke, Weimar | 1939 - 1945 | 1,000,000 | (8,3%) |
| Steyr-Daimler-Puch, Steyr | 1939 - 1945 | 828,000 | (6,9%) |
| Waffen Werke Brünn, Bystrica | 1942 - 1945 | 809,000 | (6,7% |
| Waffen Werke Brünn, Brünn | 1943 - 1945 | 882,000 | (7,4%) |

This K98k rifle was manufactured by Steyr-Daimler-Puch in 1943; the receiver ring is marked 'bnz. 43' (# 3426l, WTS Koblenz).

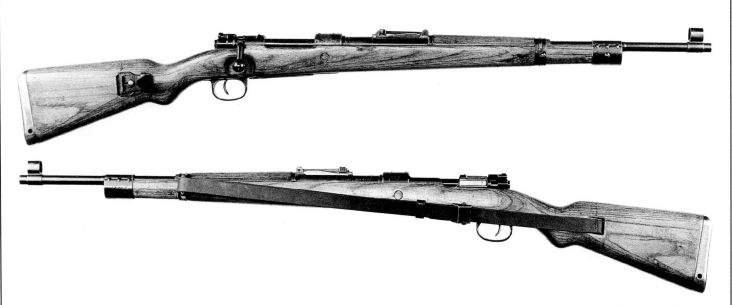

A *Kriegsmodell* K98k made by Waffenwerke Brünn in 1945. The 'Mod.98' designation stamp is located on the top of the receiver ring. Note the absence of the bayonet mount and the bolt disassembly disc. This last part was replaced by a hole drilled in the cupped buttplate (# 63900a, WTS Koblenz).

replaced other parts which were originally milled and polished as well, such as the lower and upper bands and parts of the magazine, triggerguard and loading system. Furthermore, the second scale on the underside of the backsight was eliminated, as well as the holding spring between the upper and lower band, which was thereafter fitted with screws. The traditional rust blueing was replaced by phosphating, which was cheaper, faster and very durable.

In late 1944, the so-called *Kriegsmodell* (war model: this was not an offical designation) went into production. This model was the result of an eleventh-hour simplification program, initiated in late 1943. The K98k *Kriegsmodell* lacked a bayonet lug and cleaning rod. Instead, the front of the stock was covered by a sheet metal plate. The bolt guide lug and the bolt disassembly disc were discontinued, the latter replaced by a hole in the side of the butt cap. In some cases the rear sight was replaced by a stamped, non-adjustable fixed sight. Most of these weapons were also provided with a boring at the barrel muzzle to prevent bulging.

Despite all simplifications, the K98k *Kriegsmodell* performed as well as 1935 production weapons, for only components that had no influence on shooting performance were modified or omitted.

The last step in this continuing process was the K98kv ('v' for *vereinfacht*, simplified). The K98kv was a Mauser design, featuring a K98k mechanism with a straight bolt handle and a new sight, ranging from 100 to 500 m. It was fitted with a one-piece, sheet-metal, floorplate-magazine, housing-enlarged trigger guard assembly. Many other internal parts were of sheet metal as well. The stock was shortened to 74 cm, the handguard omitted and the design of the firing pin was modified. It seems that no specimen of the K98kv, developed in the very last months of the war, has survived(6).

Despite rationalization of the arms industry and simplification of the K98k design and production process, demands were never fully met. The main reason for persistant shortages was the heavy losses of small arms. Between September 1, 1939, and February, 1945, more than six million K98k's were reported missing (lost, broken or captured). Due to the race between production and losses, the German army never exceeded an amount of six million K98k's in its inventory. This figure was reached in early 1942, just before the Russian victory at Stalingrad(7).

## The K98k for the SS

The notorious SS began as a small organization in the early thirties, but it developed into a 100,000 man army (*Waffen-SS*: armed SS) in early 1940, finally to become nearly a one million man army by 1944. The military successes and continuous expansion of the SS reflected its increasing political influence, as was clearly demonstrated by the methods in which the SS acquired its armament.

Initially, the SS was mainly armed with former World War I and *Reichswehr* weapons (K98a, K98b, Gewehr 98) and 'commercial' Mauser *Standard Modell* rifles, many of which were converted to the K98k configuration, probably mostly by Erma. This situation soon changed, and thereafter the SS was supplied with newly manufactured K98k's.

However, the SS also had its own source of supply, probably the ultimate in cynism. In 1943, the concentration camps of Buchenwald and Mauthausen, controlled by the SS as all others, were involved in the production of the K98k. The Buchenwald assembly line was supervised by Gustloff Werke, while Steyr controlled the works in Mauthausen. It is reported that the Dachau concentration camp was used to assemble K98k's as well. In total, some 150,000 to 200,000 K98k rifles were made in the concentration camps.

Mauser's Oberndorf plant manufactured approximately 4,400,000 K98k's. This specimen, marked 'byf 45', was made in the last months of the war (# 38089, WTS Koblenz).

This K98k is a mystery. It is stamped with several SS-runes and swastikas on the receiver ring and barrel; the other markings (see page 49), the enlarged trigger guard and the grasping grooves are most unusual as well. Everything indicates this weapon is a fake, apart from the fact that it was kept in an official collection for several decades (# 6046, MoD Pattern Room Nottingham).

# III  THE K98k SNIPER RIFLE

## Too little and too late

Contrary to popular belief, the German army was not very interested in snipers and sniper weapons at the dawn of World War II. In 1934, one year before the adoption of the K98k, sniper equipment was even officially discarded. In 1938, however, when Hitler's massive rearmament program was fully implemented, this measure was revoked. Interest in sniper weapons nevertheless remained low, until experiences of war forced the army command to a new approach.

The first requests from troops for more sniper rifles came after the invasion of Poland, but the problem became really pressing in the second half of 1941. Although the campaign against the Soviet Union was very successful in the beginning, the German war machine was soon halted by the severe Russian winter. Moreover, the Red army had reorganized its defenses and was employing increasing numbers of well-trained marksman with very effective sniper rifles, who took a heavy toll.

To counteract the Russian snipers, the German army was in desperate need of K98k sniper rifles, but production of this type of weapon was initially very low. Due to a lack of suitable equipment, German soldiers were eager to use captured Russian sniper rifles (Mosin Nagant bolt action rifles and Simonov and Tokarev semi-automatic rifles). The shortages were also partially supplemented with the reissue of W.W.I *Gewehr 98* sniper rifles and other irregular arms, but this was just a drop in the ocean as well.

From late 1941 onward, an increasing number of K98k's were equipped with a newly adopted telescopic sight, the ZF41. This device however, had only a 1.5-fold magnification and was useless even for medium range. Other service models were developed, but a single

system was never adopted. Finally, a bewildering variety of mountings and sights were used. This extremely varied collection of commercial and service types remained in use until the very last days of the war. K98k rifles that were used for sniping were of normal manufacture. They were selected for sniping afterwards, by a series of test shots with and without telescopic sights. The trigger mechanism of selected weapons was often tuned to a pull of 1.5 kg to 2.5 kg. Furthermore, the barrel bedding was checked to ensure that the barrel did not touch the stock. Although other weapons, in particular the semi-automatic Gewehr 43, were also fitted with telescopic sights, the experienced sniper always preferred the bolt-action K98k. It was more precise and far more reliable.

## The K98k sniper

German snipers were usually selected from trained marksmen such as hunters and experienced soldiers who were excellent riflemen. They had to complete a sniper course at a 'Sharpshooter Training Company', consisting of firing exercises, tactics, observation and camouflage training. Afterwards, the sniper was sent to the front, taking the K98k with telescopic sight he had trained with, with him(8).

In general, German snipers were exempt from guard and other duties, and had great liberty in selecting their targets, which were usually engaged at a distance of about 500 meters. During attack, snipers always worked in teams: one as a spotter, looking for targets with his binoculairs, the other shooting the rifle. Defensively, most snipers were on their own, especially looking out for enemy snipers, observers and commanders. Apart from the standard equipment, the

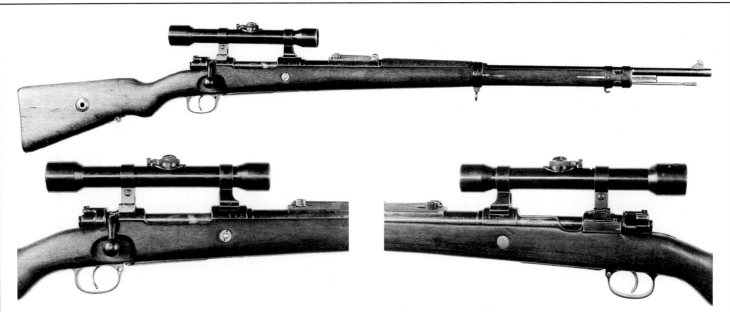

A G98 sniper rifle with curved bolt handle and a *Zielvier* telescopic sight. This specimen was converted to the sS-cartridge by Mauser in 1936-1938; the new rear sight is marked 'S/42' (# 3234B, WTS Koblenz).

A K98k with a rare, turret mounted Carl Zeiss Jena *Zielsechs* (six-fold) telescopic sight. Note the flattened safety (# 5598n, WTS Koblenz).

sniper was provided with binoculars, winter trigger, camouflage net and jacket and 90 rounds of special ammunition. This ammunition was a special issue of the SmE (Spitzgeschoss mit Eisenkern), with very good ballistic performance. In February 1945, Hitler personally allowed the use of the explosive 'Beobachtungspatrone' on the eastern front, following an unjustified claim that Soviet snipers were using such types of ammunition.

Very successful snipers were initially awarded the Iron Cross, but in the fall of 1944 the sniper's badge was introduced. It consisted of an oval badge with the head of an eagle and two oak leaves. The sniper's badge was seldom seen, however, since a sniper risked immediate execution when taken prisoner and being identified as such.

## Telescopic sights and mounting systems

German types of telescopic sights varied from 1.5 to six fold magnification and were of many different origins: commercial hunting telescopes, commercial types manufactured under military contract (ZF 39) and the officially adopted ZF41 and ZF4 (ZFK 43) models. These sights, and their respective mountings, are briefly described below(9).

The first model of telescopic sight officially adopted by the German army was the ZF39 (Zielfernrohr 1939). The designation 'model' is actually not accurate, since an official model never existed. The ZF39, commonly referred to as Zielvier, was a collective name for all fourfold magnification, commercial telescopic sights of many different models, produced by numerous optical firms. The ZF39 was already in use before its official adoption, but was standardized on a range graduation to 1,200 meters in 1940. In practice, this regulation was often neglected. It was mounted on at least six different types of mounts: the short and long side rail type, the

high and low turret types and single and double claw types.

The long side rail system, introduced by Gustloff Werke in early 1944, featured a unique characteristic: the K98k receiver was modified in manufacture, by fitting it with a thicker left receiver wall. This wall was then machined flat to accommodate the mount.

To meet demands for more K98k telescopic-sight sniper rifles, the army developed a new type, which was adopted in July 1941. This was the peculiar ZF41 (Zielfernrohr 1941), with a length of 13 cm featuring a 1.5-fold magnification only. It was mounted to a short dovetailed rail on the left side of the rear sight band and was positioned over the center of the bore. The ZF41 (also referred to as ZF40 and later simplified into the ZF41/1) featured an extremely long eye relief of about 30 cm. It was small, easy to mount and did not interfere with loading, but the 1.5-fold magnification made the ZF41 militarily unusable.

However, the K98k with ZF41 was never intended to be a pure sniping arm, but merely used for advanced sharpshooting. It was planned to provide 6% of all K98k's with a ZF41 mount, but this goal was never achieved. In early 1944 the K98k with ZF41 was even officially downgraded from 'telescopic rifle' to an ordinary 'Karabiner'. Despite its degradation, the ZF41 remained in use until the end.

The ZF4 telescopic sight (renamed ZFK43 and ZFK43/1) was developed for the G43 rifle and based on the Russian model, but was mounted on the K98k as well. This was mainly due to the dramatic performance of the G43, which was plagued with production problems. Moreover, it was hoped the new scope could eventually replace the commercial telescopic sights. The ZF4 was mounted on a so-called swept back mount, introduced some months before the end of the war. This mount was manufactured in limited quantity.

A double-claw mount K98k sniper, made by Mauser ('byf') and fitted with a Opticotechna ('dow') telescopic sight. Although it is reported this configuration was mostly used by the SS, this specimen does not feature any SS markings (# 15369, WTS Koblenz).

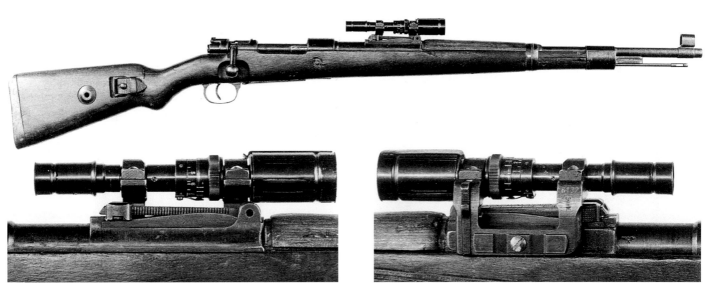

This K98k with a ZF 41/1 telescopic sight was made by Mauser at Borsigwalde. The receiver ring is marked 'ar 43' (# 3966dd, WTS Koblenz).

Reliable figures about the number of K98k's with telescopic sights are very difficult to find. The following list is based on figures from three original sources, but is still far from complete. Furthermore, the types of telescopic sights are not specified. A very rough calculation, based on these incomplete figures, indicates that approximately 200,000 K98k's with telescopic sights were manufactured. Probably about 100,000 were of the ZF41-type, while the other half consisted of the other types.

## Telescopic sight manufacturers and codes

| | |
|---|---|
| Hensoldt, Herborn | bek |
| Carl Zeiss, Jena | blc |
| Hensoldt & Söhne, Wetzlar | bmj |
| J.G. Farbenindustrie, München | bzz |
| Karl Kahles, Wien | cad |
| Swarovski, Rathenow | cag |
| Wöhler, Kassel | clb |
| Busch, Rathenow | cxn |
| Oculus, Berlin | ddv |
| Voigtländer, Braunschweig | ddx |
| Schneider & Co, Kreuznach | dkl |
| Opticotechna, Prerau | dow |
| Runge & Kaulfuss, Rathenau | dym |
| Rodenstock, München | eso |
| Spindler & Hoyer, Göttingen | fvs |
| Feinmechanik, Kassel | fzg |
| Ruf & Co, Kassel | gkp |
| Kohl AG, Chemnitz | hap |
| Ludwig, Weixdorf | jve |
| Ford Werke AG, Berlin | kay |
| Barbier, Benard et Turenne, Paris | kov |
| C.W. Crous & Co, Berga | mow |
| Carl Zeiss, Jena | rln |

## K98k with telescopic sights, October 1942 - March 1945 (10)

| Month | Year | Required | Accepted |
|---|---|---|---|
| October | 1942 | 4,000 | 3,732 |
| November | 1942 | 4,000 | 3,423 |
| December | 1942 | 4,000 | 5,771 |
| January | 1943 | 4,000 | 5,380 |
| February | 1943 | 4,150 | 5,380 |
| March | 1943 | 4,150 | 6,050 |
| April | 1943 | 4,150 | 5,030 |
| May | 1943 | 4,150 | 3,474 |
| June | 1943 | 4,000 | No figures |
| July | 1943 | 4,000 | 5,288 |
| August | 1943 | 4,150 | 4,797 |
| September | 1943 | 4,650 | 3,605 |
| October | 1943 | 4,650 | No figures |
| November | 1943 | 4,650 | No figures |
| December | 1943 | 4,650 | 4,906 |
| January | 1944 | 4,650 | No figures |
| February | 1944 | 4,650 | No figures |
| March | 1944 | 4,650 | No figures |
| April | 1944 | 4,650 | 3,276 |
| May | 1944 | 6,000 | No figures |
| June | 1944 | 9,000* | No figures |
| July | 1944 | 12,000* | No figures |
| August | 1944 | 15,000* | No figures |
| September | 1944 | 18,000* | No figures |
| October | 1944 | 20,000* | 1,984 |
| November | 1944 | 6,000 | 3,900 |
| December | 1944 | 6,000 | 2,533 |
| January | 1945 | 6,000 | 1,775 |
| February | 1945 | 6,000 | 1,296 |
| March | 1945 | 6,000 | 912 |

* These figures were shortly afterwards lowered to 6.000 a month, while the required amounts of K43 with telescopic sights was heightened.

This Gustloff K98k sniper (marked 'bcd 4') has a special enlarged receiver machined flat to accommodate the long side-rail mount. The weapon is fitted with a Dialytan telescopic sight ('bek': Hensoldt, Herborn) and a lengthened safety (# 26081, WTS Koblenz).

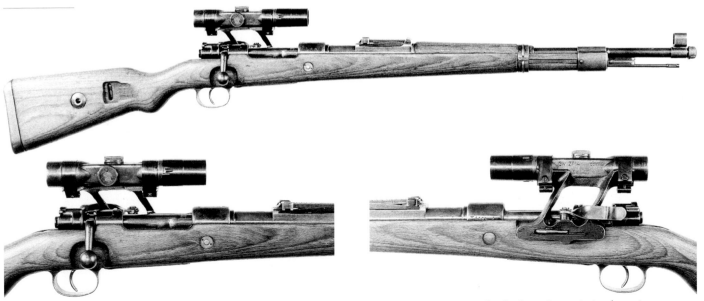

The ZF 4 sight (also designated ZFK43 & ZFK43/1) on the rare swept-back mount. The locking lever is in the release position. This K98k is marked 'CE 44' and was made by Sauer & Sohn (# 1104l, WTS Koblenz).

# IV K98k VARIATIONS

## Experimental models

Apart from the standard K98k model, some experimental versions were made. The first was the so-called G40k (*Gewehr 40 kurz*), developed by Mauser on request of the infantry arms development and research department (*Wa Prüf 2*). Between 1940 and mid-1942, about thirty weapons of this type were made, featuring a K98k mechanism with a 49 cm barrel. The K98k-type stock was shortened and had a single upper band only, with a swiveling front sling mount and no cleaning rod. The rear sight was shortened and a hole was drilled into the knob of the bolt handle. Apparently, the G40k project was initiated to develop a shorter, easy to manufacture K98 variant, but it was abandoned without any noticeable result.

To facilitate transport of the K98k, at least two special 'break-down' models were designed, probably intended for paratroop or commando units. The first type was provided with a detachable barrel. Just in front of the receiver, the barrel the front part of the stock and the handguard could be detached by disengaging a locking bar and turning the barrel assembly. The other model featured a folding stock, with a hinge behind the trigger guard. Only very few of both types were made.

Another rare modified K98k was the grenade launching rifle, featuring a grenade launcher permanently attached to its shortened barrel, a MG34 bipod and a modified butt. This variation was probably an experiment by a local gunsmith, just like the rare K98k's modified to fire flare cartridges.

## Training and education rifles

For training and education, there was the cutaway rifle. It was produced in several versions, with small differences. The cutaway version was mainly used to demonstrate the functioning of the mechanism and to show the internal components without disassembling the rifle.

The *Kleinkaliber-Wehrsportgewehr* ('KKW': small caliber military and sporting rifle) was a .22 LR training rifle, closely resembling the K98k. These weapons were introduced in the Weimar era, to promote and stimulate shooting exercises without violating the Treaty of Versailles. There were many manufacturers, producing several models with small differences. During the war, the .22 rifles were used for preliminary shooting education to the *Hitler-Jugend* and other auxiliary forces. The ammunition was cheap and could be used on every indoor range*(11)*.

## Export K98k's

Traditionally, China was the most important market for Mauser-type rifles and carbines. From the 1880's onward, the Chinese acquired great amounts of weapons from Germany, Czechoslovakia and Belgium. Mauser delivered an unknown quantity (probably a few hundred thousand) of *Standard Modell* and K98k rifles to China, often marked with the Mauser banner and Chinese proof and acceptance marks. These deliveries ended shortly after the Japanese invasion of China, in the summer of 1937. Some of the exported K98k's were assembled from parts rejected by the German army.

A second Asian customer for K98k's was Japan, which

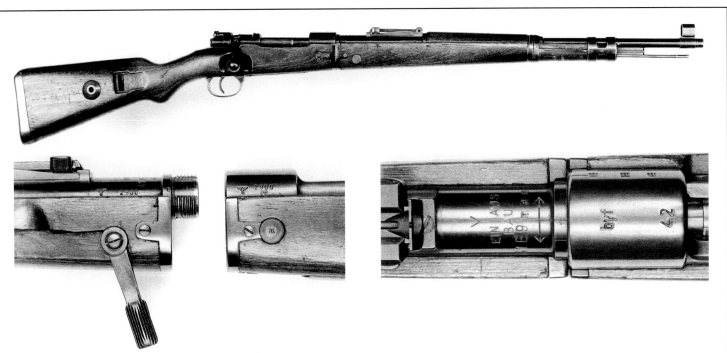

The detachable barrel K98k was a Mauser experimental development for paratrooper use. To detach the barrel, the lever was swung, the barrel turned 90° to the right and subsequently removed from the receiver. Note the text *Ein - Aus Bau*, respectively meaning attach and detach (# 2900u, MoD Pattern Room, Nottingham).

A second experimental Mauser K98k (marked '42 1938') was this folding-stock rifle, with a hinge behind the trigger guard. This is probably the only specimen that has survived (# 7146u, MoD Pattern Room Nottingham).

ordered 20,000 K98k's in early 1937. Apart from the Mauser banner on the stock, these K98k's were similar to the German version. Portugal acquired K98k's as well, which are easily distinguishable by the Portuguese crest on the receiver. Some of these weapons were diverted to the German army. Sweden acquired 2,500 K98k's in 1939. The Swedish rifles, designated M40, fired the 8 x 63 mm cartridge and featured a special muzzle break. Finally, there were limited deliveries to Germany's allies, Bulgaria and Croatia, during the war: Croatia acquired 7,000 K98k's in the autumn of 1944; Bulgaria is reported to have had 18,000 rifles in 1943.

## Foreign weapons

Besides the K98k, the German army used many other rifles and carbines. For the most part, these were captured foreign rifles or foreign models, produced under German occupation. Usually, such weapons were issued to specific units, such as police troops and auxiliary forces. However, some foreign weapons were used more extensively by 'normal' German army units and these rifles and carbines are described here.

The G29/40 rifle was the German designation for the modified Polish model wz29 rifle. Except for the position of the sling swivels, this weapon was basically identical to the K98k. When the German Army occupied Poland, a large quantity of these weapons were captured, restocked and subsequently reissued. In addition to their Polish markings, these weapons were also stamped with '660' (the Steyr-code) and the year of conversion on the receiver ring. Afterwards, the assembly line was transferred to Steyr, where production was continued.

The G29/40 can be identified by the marking '29/40' on the left side of the receiver wall. Polish-made weapons also feature the Polish eagle on the receiver, and the letters 'wz' (the Polish abbreviation for model) preceding the designation. Usually, these letters were overstruck and sometimes a 'G' was added, thus changing "wz29" into G29/40.

The G33/40 was a former Czechoslovakian 16/33 carbine, featuring a 49 cm barrel. Unlike the Polish G29/40, the Czech G33/40 remained in production during the war. In German service, the G33/40 was mostly used by mountain troops. For this purpose it was fitted with a cupped buttplate and a protective metal panel on the left side of the butt.

The Gewehr 24(t) was the former Czech Vz24 standard army rifle. It was fitted with an upper handguard extending to the receiver ring, a bolt with a straight handle, and bottom- and side-mounted sling swivels. The German army acquired many Vz24's from pre-war production, but continued manufacture during the occupation as well. Most German-produced weapons feature a bolt disassembly disc, a slot in the stock for the German sling and often a cupped buttplate. The Czech marking disk on the right side of the stock was omitted.

Despite its designation, the G98/40 rifle was not a Mauser, but a modified Hungarian Mannlicher Model 35. Originally chambered for the Hungarian 8 x 56 mm rimmed cartridge, the chamber was reamed out to fit the German ammunition and a thumb slot was cut into the left receiver wall. Furthermore, the magazine and the receiver bridge were modified so the weapon could be loaded with Mauser clips. Finally, a new sight and a K98k bayonet lug were added and the sling attachment was relocated to the left side of the stock.

The so-called *Luftwaffen-Karabiner* is probably the most

This K98k was made for Portugal, but used by the German army. It features Portuguese K98k characteristics as the guarded front sight, the Portuguese crest on the receiver ring and different sling swivels, but German 'WaA63' *Abnahme* markings as well (# D17439, MoD Pattern Room Nottingham).

A former Polish Wz29 rifle, converted by Steyr into a German G29/40. The receiver ring of this weapon features the Polish crest and the text *F.B. Radom*, with '660' and '1939' added later (# 5235A, WTS Koblenz).

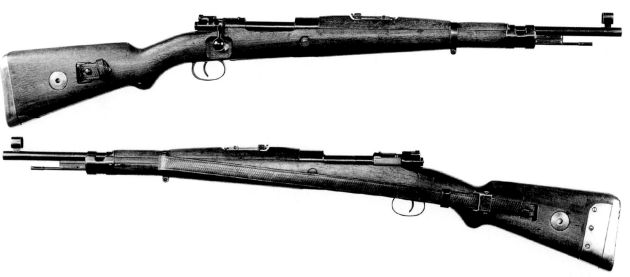

This G33/40 was made by Brno ('945 1940' on the receiver ring) and fitted with a protective metal panel on the left side of the butt. It was used by Mountain Troops (# 4053, WTS Koblenz).

mysterious of all K98k variations. Externally, it resembles the Vz24 in many details. It features a long handguard, a marking disk in the bolt and a lower barrel band with sling swivels on the bottom and on the left side. However, all specimens found are marked '660' and 1938 or 1939 and bear *Luftwaffe* markings. The weapon was thus made in the Steyr plant, shortly after the *Anschluss* with Germany, and used by the *Luftwaffe*. Although evidence is lacking, it is believed that this weapon was intended to become the new Austrian army rifle, just before Austria ceased to exist. When the *Luftwaffe* found out about the new weapon, it immediately since the opportunity to acquire this batch of modern rifles, since the army received nearly all newly produced K98k's.

Many other captured foreign rifles were used by the regular German army and auxiliary troops as well. The most important types are listed with their German designation.

| Rifle type and country | German designation |
| --- | --- |
| Krag Jorgensen M.94 (Norway) | G.211(n) |
| Krag Jorgensen M.89 (Denmark) | G.311(d) |
| Lebel M86/93 (France) | G.301(f) |
| Lee Enfield No. 1 MkIII (UK) | G.281(e) |
| Mannlicher Carcano M.91 (Italy) | G.214(i) |
| Mannlicher M.95 (Holland) | G.211(h) |
| Mannlicher M.95 (Austria) | G.95(ö) |
| Mannlicher M.03 14 (Greece) | G.215(g) |
| MAS 36 (France) | G.242(f) |
| Mauser M.89 (Belgium) | G.261(b) |
| Mauser M.36 (Belgium) | G.263(b) |
| Mosin Nagant 91/30 (Russia) | G.254(r) |

The Czech Vz24 rifle remained in production during the occupation. Unlike pre-war weapons, this German G24(t) (marked 'dou 41') was fitted with a bolt disassembly disc and a slot in the stock for the German sling (# 6146, WTS Koblenz).

This G98/40 is a modified, former Hungarian Mannlicher Model 35. Note the German sling attachment and the K98k bayonet lug (# 3741, WTS Koblenz).

The mysterious *Luftwaffe Karabiner*. It is believed this weapon was intended to become the new Austrian army rifle, just before the *Anschluss* with Germany. (# 3880, MoD Pattern Room Nottingham).

# V TECHNICAL DESCRIPTION

## The Mauser 98 mechanism

The main parts of the Mauser K98k are the receiver, the magazine and trigger assembly and the bolt (13). The barrel is screwed into the front side of the one-piece receiver. Inside the receiver ring is a collar, which extends around the inside of the ring and surrounds the bolt head when the bolt is closed. The rear of the left receiver wall has a thumb recess, to aid loading the magazine with the clip. This is the only major weak point of the K98k, since the left side of the receiver tends to crack when dropped on a hard surface.

The rear of the receiver consists of a grooved tang, which accepts the cocking piece cam, and the receiver bridge, which is slotted on the top front side for the clip. On the left side of the receiver bridge is the bolt stop, which protrudes through a hole under the bridge to halt the rearward motion of the bolt when it is drawn back. In front of the bolt stop, and also projecting through a hole in the receiver bridge, is the ejector.

The bottom of the receiver is milled to form the magazine well, with lips at both sides of the upper edges to hold the cartridges. Underneath the receiver is the one-piece magazine and trigger guard assembly.

The trigger mechanism consists of the sear, the trigger (with two humps on top to provide the two-stage trigger pull) and the trigger spring. The sear is hinged under the rear of the receiver, while the trigger is hinged to the sear. The sear and the trigger are tensioned by the trigger spring, recessed at the front of the sear.

The bolt consists of the body with an integral bent-down bolt handle with a knob, the extractor, the bolt sleeve, the cocking piece, the safety, the coil mainspring and the firing pin. The bolt is bored from the rear to accept the main spring and the firing pin. On the front end of the bolt are two locking lugs, of which the right one is solid and the left one slotted to allow the ejector to pass through. A third lug is located at the rear, in line with the right front locking lug. The top of the bolt body is provided with a guide rib, which was omitted in the latter part of the war. On the underside of the bolt body there are two oblong vents, to allow powder gases to escape in the event of a ruptured case or a pierced primer.

The bolt head has a hole for the firing pin and a rim about two-thirds around the bolt head. A part of this rim, through which the ejector slot passes, is made higher. This small projection assists in holding the cartridge, when it is grasped by the opposed extractor hook. The extractor is attached to the bolt by a collar, which fits a groove cut into the bolt body. To prevent longitudinal movement, the extractor is also fitted with a lip, which engages a groove in the bolt head in front of the lugs.

The bolt sleeve has a hole for the rear half of the firing pin, which features two flattened sides, and is fitted to the rear side of the bolt by means of buttress threads. The rear end of the firing pin and the cocking piece are provided with three interrupted lugs. They are attached to each other by a quarter-turn. The mainspring is compressed between the flange of the firing pin and the front of the bolt sleeve. The safety is located in a hole in the top of the bolt sleeve. It is provided with a stem which extends forward through the bolt sleeve to intersect the rear of the bolt body. In

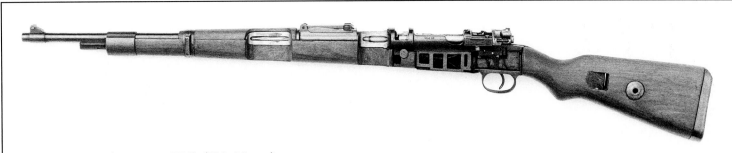

An instructional cutaway K98k (H.L. Visser)

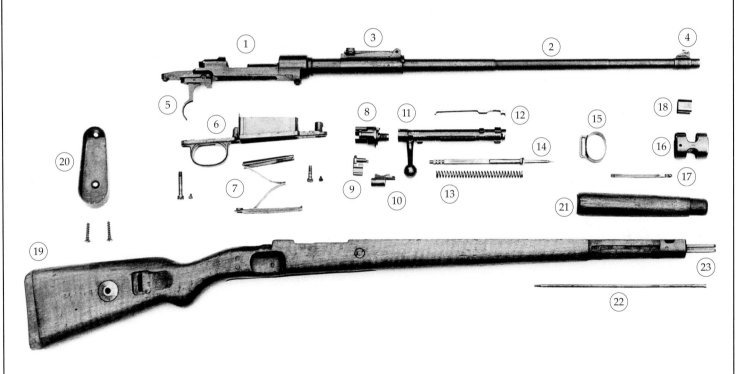

| 1 | Receiver | 9 | Safety | 17 | Band spring |
|---|---|---|---|---|---|
| 2 | Barrel | 10 | Cocking piece | 18 | Front sight hood |
| 3 | Rear sight | 11 | Bolt | 19 | Stock |
| 4 | Front sight | 12 | Extractor | 20 | Buttplate |
| 5 | Trigger | 13 | Mainspring | 21 | Handguard |
| 6 | Magazine & triggerguard | 14 | Firing pin | 22 | Cleaning rod |
| 7 | Magazine spring & follower | 15 | Lower band | 23 | Bayonet mount |
| 8 | Bolt sleeve | 16 | Upper band | | |

the safe position, with the wing swung to the far right, the notched end of the stem engages in the notch in the bolt, locking the bolt, firing pin and cocking piece.

## Operation

Starting with an empty magazine, the operation is as follows. The bolt handle is rotated 90 degrees and pulled back until halted by the bolt stop. By raising the bolt handle, the mainspring is partially cocked. Insert a loaded clip into the charger guideway of the receiver bridge and push the cartridges with the thumb into the magazine.

Then push the bolt forward. The top cartridge in the magazine is now pushed into the chamber, while on the final movement of the bolt the extractor hook grasps the cartridge base. While the bolt is rotated to the locked position, it is pulled forward by the locking lugs engaging in their recesses, while the sear engages the cocking piece to hold it back. By this movement, the mainspring is fully cocked.

When the trigger is pulled, the hinged sear is pulled down, thus releasing the cocking piece. Under tension of the mainspring, the firing pin moves forward and ignites the primer.

When the shot is fired and the bolt is moved backwards again, the empty case is pulled out the chamber by the extractor. Just before the final backward movement of the bolt, the case is pushed out the right side of the receiver by the ejector, protruding through a hole in the receiver bridge. If there are cartridges left in the magazine, the operation can be repeated. However, if the magazine is empty, the bolt is halted in its forward movement by the magazine follower. This is a safety measure to inform the shooter that the magazine is empty.

## Field stripping

Open the bolt to check the chamber and magazine. Close the bolt and place the safety in the upright position. Raise the bolt handle, pull out the near end of the bolt stop and draw the bolt from the receiver. To disassemble the bolt, depress the bolt sleeve lock plunger and unscrew the bolt sleeve and firing mechanism. Place the firing pin tip in the bolt disassembly disc and press the bolt sleeve down, then turn the cocking piece one-quarter to the left or the right and lift it off the firing pin: the mainspring can now be separated from the firing pin. The safety can be removed from the bolt sleeve by swinging it to the right and pulling it out rearward. To remove the extractor, lift the hook end away from the bolt and turn it to the bottom: then push it forward. Reassemble the bolt in reverse order.

To strip the K98k further, unscrew the rear and front triggerguard screw, and remove the one-piece magazine and trigger guard assembly. The floorplate, follower and spring can be removed. Then depress the band spring and remove first the upper, then the lower band. The handguard, barrel and receiver can now be taken apart. Reassemble in reverse order.

[1] The bolt is closed, the safety is in the off position and the cocking piece is not cocked.

[2] The bolt is pulled back and the mainspring has been partially cocked. Note the cocking piece protruding from the bolt sleeve.

[3] The bolt has been pushed forward, but not closed yet. Note the guide rib and the extractor.

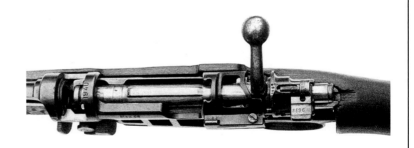

[4] The bolt is rotated and locked. The sear has engaged the cocking piece to hold it back, while the locking lugs pull the bolt fully forward to lock. Note the firing pin under tension of the mainspring.

# VI ACCESSORIES & AMMUNITION

## Ammunition pouches

The standard ammunition pouches, standardized in 1934, consisted of a three-part leather pouch, each with three 5 round clips of ammunition, thus containing 45 rounds of ammunition. Apart from some special units or second rank troops, riflemen were issued two sets of pouches. Standard ammunition pouches were colored black and dark brown, but there were also natural leather-colored and white-painted versions, for tropical conditions and winter use respectively. *Fallschirmjäger* (paratroopers) were issued cloth bandoleers, which were carried vertically and contained 100 rounds.

## Cleaning device model 34

The first K98k accessory, adopted with the introduction of the K98k, was the cleaning device model 34 (*Reinigungsgerät 34* or RG34). This item consisted of a round-sided tin box with two internal compartments. One compartment was for cleaning patches, while the other held a cylindrical oiler, a chamber brush, a bore brush, a floorplate takedown tool and a linked aluminum cleaning chain.

As with the K98k, the RG34 was simplified several times during the war, and therefore there are some variants. The first model, adopted in 1934, featured a machined steel oiler. From about 1939 onward, a bakelite oiler was used, while in 1944 a sheet-metal version was introduced. The other parts were of a more crude finish and made of inferior materials as well.

## Bayonets: the SG94/98 and the SG42

The K98k bayonet (*Seitengewehr*) was officially designated SG94/98. It featured a blade of 25 cm, an overall length of 38.5 cm and was issued with a sheet metal scabbard. Early bayonets were fitted with wooden grip panels, but later issue types often had ribbed bakelite handles. The manufacturer's code or name was stamped on the blade above the crossguard. Several millions of this type were produced.

Besides the standard SG94/98, a second model was also adopted, but manufactured on a very limited scale only. This was the SG42 of which about 2,000 were made. The SG42 was developed by the firm of Eickhorn at the request of the Ordnance department, which was looking for a multi-functional field knife. Several companies offered a design, and Eickhorn's model was selected. The SG42 was a combination of bayonet, field knife and multi-purpose tool. The tool was housed in the hollow handle, and featured a screwdriver, corkscrew, bottle-opener, knife and bradawl. The SG42 featured an overall length of 30 cm and a blade of 17.6 cm. All remaining specimens are marked 'cof' on the top of the blade, the code for Eickhorn.

## Muzzle covers

The early metal muzzle/front sight cover, adopted with the weapon, was identical to the World War I type. It consisted of a tube with a hinged muzzle cover, attached to a sight guard. The sight guard hooked behind the back side of the front sight, and was attached or removed by pressure on the muzzle cover and rotation of the complete part.

After adopting the front sight hood, in late December 1939, this model would no longer fit and was replaced by a simple rubber muzzle cap, of which four were

The round-sided tin box of the cleaning device 34 with its contents. From left to right: chamber brush, bore brush, linked aluminum chain, floorplate takedown tool and machined metal oiler (D.J. Hueting).

The rare SG42 (right) was a combination bayonet, field-knife and multi-purpose tool. It was developed and manufactured by the firm of Eickhorn (H.L. Visser).

The standard issue SG94/98 (left). This specimen features ribbed bakelite grip panels and a sheet-metal sheet (D.J. Hueting).

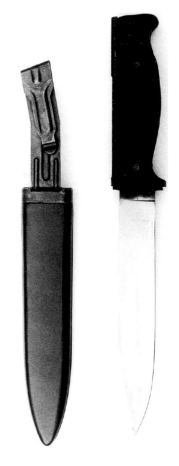

issued per rifle. The new muzzle cap was far cheaper, and in emergency situations the weapon could be fired with a muzzle cap in place.

## Sub-Caliber Conversion Unit .22

Although there were several models of .22 training rifles, a sub-caliber conversion kit was used as well. The most common model (*Einstecklauf Modell 24*: sub-caliber barrel Model 1924) was made by Erma and consisted of a wooden chest, containing a bolt, receiver and sub-caliber barrel assembly, a magazine-floorplate insert, an installation tool and two 10-round detachable box magazines. It is not known on what scale this expensive unit was used.

## Winter trigger

A winter trigger arrangement (*Winterabzug*) was developed in 1942, but only offically adopted in 1944. It consisted of an oval sheet-metal box with a lever inside, positioned in front of the trigger. By rotating the external button backwards, the internal lever depressed the trigger. The K98k winter trigger could also be used on the G98/40, G33/40, G29/40 and G29 rifles and carbines. It is not known to exactly what scale this device was distributed, but it was standard issue for snipers.

## Silencers

It is reported that a K98k silencer (*Schalldämpfer*) designated 'HUB-23,' was adopted in the second half of the war, but there seem to be no official German documents to confirm this claim. According to some sketches, this type of silencer was attached to the bayonet lug.

However, several other excavated specimens do exist.

Both types pictured here feature a two-piece hinged base that mounts around the barrel, similar to the rifle grenade launcher 42. A German author refers to the right type as 'T1', while he claims a shorter silencer of the same construction was designated 'T2'(14). The silencer on the left features the spiral design. It is reported that silencers of this construction were used on the K98k, but more detailed information is lacking.

All types of silencers fired special subsonic ammunition. These cartridges had a reduced range, due to the smaller amount of propellant, and were marked with a green bullet tip and a green cartridge base. It seems that silencers were particularly used by Paratroops, but they are very rare items of which only very few seem to have survived.

## Grenade launchers and rifle grenades

Two types of grenade launchers were used for the K98k. The first model was designated *Gewehrgranatgerät zur Panzerbekampfung 40* (GG/P40: grenade launcher for antitank use). It was attached to the rifle with the bayonet lug, whereafter the antitank rifle grenade was slid over the barrel extension. It was used with a special rear sight, a separate piece which was clamped around the stock and barrel. The GG/P40 was lighter and more compact than the second type and was intended for paratroopers. Surviving specimens are very rare.

The second model was adopted in 1942 and designated *Gewehrgranatgerät 42*. It featured a grenade launcher with a two-piece hinged base, that mounted around the barrel. The rear sight was a separate piece, incorporating a bubble level, that was attached to the rifle by means of a clamping ring. Due to complaints about this sight, it was advised in August 1944 to fire

A winter trigger mounted on a sniper rifle. An internal lever operates the trigger when the external lever is rotated backwards (MoD Pattern Room Nottingham).

Two types of excavated K98k silencers. The one on the left has a length of 25.5 cm and is marked '286'; the other features an overall length of 23 cm and bears no visible marking at all (WTS Koblenz).

The early-issue flip-up metal muzzle cover and front sight guard. This specimen is a commercial version, with a Mauser 'banner' on front (H.L. Visser).

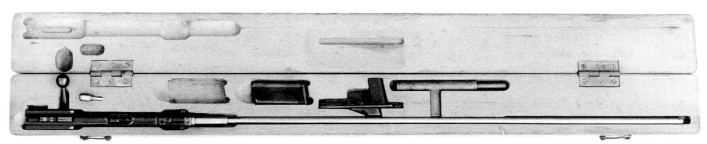

This subcaliber unit was made by Erma and designated *Einstecklauf 24* (sub-caliber barrel 24). The chest contains a bolt, inner receiver and sub-caliber barrel, two magazines (one is missing), floorplate insert and an installation tool (D.J. Hueting).

the device without the sight, until a better solution was developed. Finally, a simple launcher sight was used, but only on a very limited scale. This was the *Visierstange für das Gewehrgranatgerät 30*, consisting of a rod sight, which was clamped around the upper band.

The *Gewehrgranatgerät 42* fired several types of rifle grenades. The most common were the *Gewehrspreng-granate* (explosive rifle grenade); an improved version with extended range (*gesteigerter Reichweite*); a further improved version with extended range and special igniter (*Allseitzünder*) and four types of anti-tank rifle grenades (*Gewehrpanzergranaten*), designated model 30, 40, 46 and 61. The first two types were standard anti-tank rifle grenades; both last models featured the hollow-charge design. Furthermore, there were several types for practice and some special types of rifle grenades for illumination, smoke and propaganda.

## Curved barrel attachment

Development of this device started in 1941, to facilitate test firing with fixed aircraft machine guns. Shortly afterwards, Rheinmetall Börsig began to adapt the concept of the *Krummlauf* to the K98k, to allow the rifle to be fired from a covered position. In the autumn of 1943 two versions were tested, with 30 and 90 degree curved barrels. For the 7.9 x 57 mm ammunition, the first type proved to be the most suitable. It was mounted to the barrel by means of the same mechanism as the grenade launcher 42.

After a few prototypes for the K98k had been made, however, development of a curved barrel attachment was concentrated on the *Sturmgewehr*. This assault rifle was intended to become the future German standard rifle, while its 7.9 x 33 mm short cartridge was more suitable for the *Krummlauf*.

## Ammunition

In 1917 the 'sS-Patrone' (*schweres Spitzgeschoss*; heavy pointed bullet) was introduced for machineguns, but in the early thirties it was adopted as the standard ammunition for all 7.92 x 57 mm small arms. The sS-cartridge featured a longer, heavier bullet (35.3 mm) than its predecessor with the S-bullet. It was slower at the start, but at long range it hits the target with more energy. Another advantage of the longer bullet was that it facilitated development of special types of ammunition.

To identify the different ammunition types, color codes were used. The colors were applied on the primer or the primer annulus, as a colored band on the cartridge base, on the bullet (tip, half, complete or band), or at the case mouth. There are some general rules for these color codes. Ammunition for tropical use, especially made for the Afrika Korps, has a colored case mouth in the same colour as the primer annulus. Improved types of ammunition, usually with a modified load for greater velocity and to be used in machine guns, were marked with a green band near the bullet tip.

The headstamp of the cartridge case (cases may be encountered in brass, copper-washed steel or lacquered steel) offers information on the origin: the manufacturer, the date and lot of production and the case material. The manufacturer's code is at the 12 o'clock position; the material of the case at three o'clock; the manufacturing lot at six o'clock; and the year of manufacture at nine o'clock. The manu-facturer's code was changed several times. First it consisted of a letter 'P' with a number, later this became first a two-letter and finally a three-letter code.

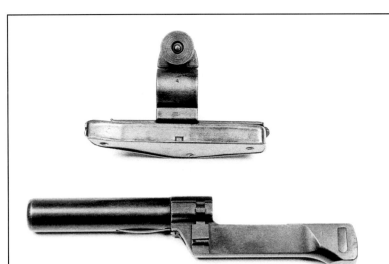

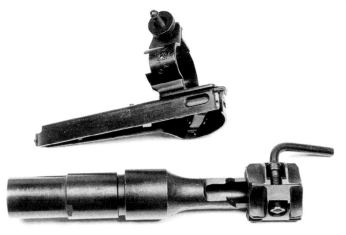

The GG/P40 rifle grenade launcher for paratroopers with its special sight. Note the folded-down auxiliary front sight in the center section of the launcher and the small *Luftamt* mark on top of the back sight (MoD Pattern Room Nottingham).

The standard issue *Gewehrgranat Gerät 42* with its sight. The grenade launcher features a two-piece hinged base, that mounted around the barrel (MoD Pattern Room Nottingham).

The GG/P40 rifle grenade launcher mounted on a K98k (MoD Pattern Room Nottingham).

A K98k with 30 degree curved barrel attachment, as it was tested in 1943. Afterward, the *Krummlauf* was developed further for the Sturmgewehr (MoD Pattern Room Nottingham).

The main types of 7.92 x 57 mm cartridges, as used in the K98k, are listed briefly below.

**Heavy ball** (*schweres Spitzgeschoss*) During World War II the standard ammunition for all German 7.92 x 57 mm caliber small arms. Primer annulus black up to 1930, green afterwards.

**Semi-armor piercing** (*Spitzgeschoss mit Eisenkern*) This cartridge features a 37.3 mm projectile with a metal core, designed to spare strategic materials. Primer annulus blue. A version with a longer bullet (39.6 mm) exists as well.

**Armor-piercing** (*Spitzgeschoss mit Kern*) Cartridge with a bullet with a steel core in a lead sleeve and a gilding-metal jacket. Red primer annulus.

**Improved armor-piercing** (*Spitzgeschoss mit Hartkern*) Later type armor piercing cartridge with a bullet-core of tungsten carbide. Annulus or entire primer painted red.

**Armor-piercing tracer** (*Spitzgeschoss mit Kern, Leuchtspur*) Bullet with steel core and a tracer element at the rear. Red primer annulus and a 10 mm black bullet tip.

**Armor-piercing incendiary** (*Phosphor mit Kern*) Bullet with steel core and phosphorous component at the rear. Red band across cartridge base, later only black primer annulus.

**Ball, reduced load** (*Nahpatrone*) This cartridge featured a reduced load to keep its velocity under 300 m/s and was used with silenced weapons. Green-painted case.

**Observation cartridge** (*Beobachtungspatrone*) This explosive incendiary cartridge, usually called 'B-patrone', was manufactured in two versions. The first type had a 10 mm silver bullet tip, the second version had the lower half of the bullet blackened. Both types had a black primer annulus.

**Blank, Model of 1933** (*Platzpatrone 33*) Hollow wooden bullet, (usually) painted red. Reduced load of special powder.

**Dummy** (*Exerzier Patrone Spitzgeschoss*) One-piece cartridge of brass or copper-washed steel with pointed 'bullet'. The case is always fluted, the bullet sometimes also.

**Dummy, plastic** (*Exerzier Patrone Spitzgeschoss, Kunststoff*) Solid red plastic cartridge with steel base. (A similar but black colored type was used for instruction).

**Grenade cartridge** (*Gewehr-Treibpatrone*) Several versions exist, for use with different types of rifle grenades. They have either a short, wooden bullet or no bullet at all. Some types have a lengthened case.

A selection of rifle grenades for the *Gewehrgranat Gerät 42*. From left to right: *Gewehrpanzergranate* 30, 61, 46, 40, *Gewehrsprenggranate*. At the right is a cut-away of a *Gewehrsprenggranate* with a time fuse: this rifle grenade could be used as a hand grenade as well (D.J. Hueting).

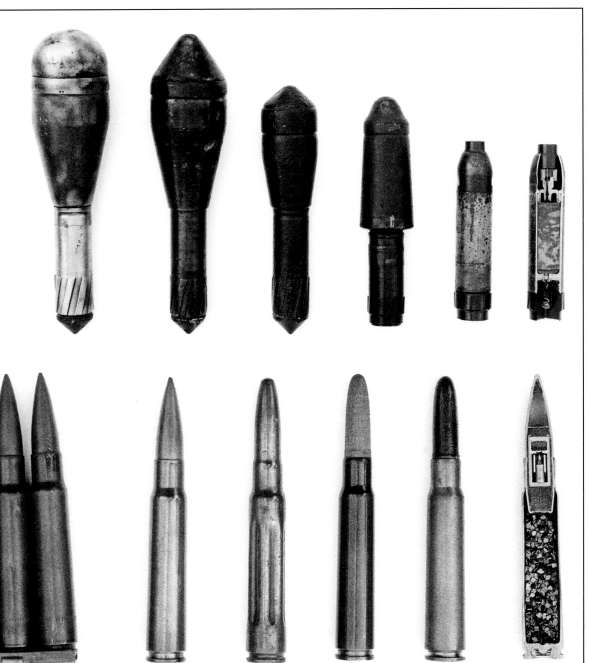

A small selection of cartridges, as used for the K98k. On the left is a clip with ball rounds. The grooved ring around the cases indicate these are reloaded. The cartridges from left to right: heavy ball, dummy, blank with lacquered steel case, blank with brass case, cut-away of an observation cartridge (D.J. Hueting).

# VII MARKINGS & CODES

## Standard markings

To identify a K98k and to retrieve its history, the codes and markings on the weapon are the most useful means. The markings on top of the receiver identify the manufacturer and the date of production, while the model designation stamp on the left side of the receiver indicates if the weapon is a newly made K98k (Mod.98), a converted *Gewehr 98* (Gew. 98) or a converted K98b (Karab.98b).

The serial number does not add much information to the receiver codes, but it is an important aid in determining the original condition, the most important characteristic for the collector. The complete number was stamped on the major components: usually the barrel, receiver, bolt and stock. The other parts were stamped with the two last digits only.

The firing proof mark was stamped on the bolt, barrel and receiver (usually left of the serial number), after the rifle had passed the test of firing two *sS Beschuss* cartridges, which produced a pressure of 4500 kg/cm2. The firing proof stamp was a small eagle, initially Weimar-style, later on in Nazi-style.

The inspection stamp indicated the inspected part had met military requirements. The stamp itself was an eagle with a number beneath, often with the letters WaA (*Wehrmachtabnahme Amt*) in front. Early production K98k's feature Weimar eagles, later versions are stamped with Nazi-style eagles. To these rules there are, of course, exceptions. Early K98k's were provided with many markings and stamps, but in the course of the war the amount diminished. In late 1944 and early 1945, firing proof stamps, inspection stamps and even serial numbers were sometimes omitted entirely.

## Special markings

Unlike World War I and the Weimar-era, small arms of the Third Reich were not provided with unit markings: "Small arms, including edged weapons, will no longer be unit-marked. Record-keeping of small arms will in the future be based on manufacturers trademarks as applied to the weapons". Due to this order in January 1934, it is virtually impossible to assign a specific weapon to a certain unit or army branch. However, some exceptions exist.

K98k stocks were usually marked with an eagle and a letter: 'H' for *Heer* (Army), 'L' for *Luftwaffe* (Airforce) and 'M' for *Marine* (Navy). Some navy stocks were also stamped 'N' or 'O', indicating *Nordseeflotte* or *Ostseeflotte* (North Sea or Baltic Sea).

**Main inspection stamps per manufacturer. Letter or WaA-prefixes are omitted.**

|  | Mauser(0) | Mauser(B) | Sauer | Erma | BLM | BSW | Gustloff | Steyr | Bystrica | Brünn |
|---|---|---|---|---|---|---|---|---|---|---|
| 1934 | 74/91 | - | 114/116 | - | - | - | - | - | - | - |
| 1935 | 167/211 | 211 | 14/116 | 132/280 | - | - | - | - | - | - |
| 1936 | 63 | 211 | 214/359 | 280 | 26 | 4 | - | - | - | - |
| 1937 | 63 | 211/280 | 214/359 | 280/77 | 26 | 4 | - | - | - | - |
| 1938 | 63 | 280 | 214/359 | 280/77 | 26 | 4 | - | - | - | - |
| 1939 | 63/655 | 26 | 359/37 | 280 | 214 | - | 4/46 | 623 | - | - |
| 1940 | 655 | 26 | 359/37 | 280 | 214 | - | 749 | 623 | - | - |
| 1941 | 655 | 26 | 359/37 | 280 | 214 | - | 749 | 623 | - | - |
| 1942 | 655/135 | 26 | 359/37 | - | 214 | - | 749 | 623 | 80 | - |
| 1943 | 135 | 26 | 359/37 | - | - | - | 749 | 623 | 80 | 63 |
| 1944 | 135 | 135/26 | 280/37 | - | - | - | 749 | 623 | 80 | 63 |
| 1945 | 135 | - | - | - | - | - | 749 | 623 | 80 | 63 |

Three model designation markings: *Gewehr 98*, Carbine 98 and K98k (Mod 98).

The firing proof mark. From left to right: Imperial style, Weimar style and Nazi style eagles.

Two inspection stamps, Weimar and Nazi style, and a *Luftwaffe* stock marking.

A Polish Wz29 transformed into a G29/40, and two markings on a *Standard Modell II* rifle (page 13, bottom). 'D.R.P.' means *Deutsche Reichs Post* (German Postal Service), 'Dtmd' stands for the city of Dortmund.

The other exception is an unknown quantity of K98k's used by the SS. These weapons are stamped with SS runes and the Death's head, usually on the barrel and stock, and feature the commercial firing proof mark as well: a crowned letter 'N'. Other SS markings consist of the letters 'SSZZA', followed by a letter. This is an abbreviation for *SS Zentral Zeug Amt* (SS Central Ordnance Depot). These markings are also found on (converted) Gewehr 98's with and without mount and telescopic sight, since these weapons were initially acquired by the SS.

Finally, there is an unknown quantity of Steyr-made K98k's, marked with a single rune beneath the 'bnz' code, which were assembled in the Mauthausen concentration camp.

## The receiver code

As mentioned before, the markings on top of the receiver identify the manufacturer and the date of production. The only exceptions to this rule are the Gustloff Werke and Steyr-Daimler-Puch made weapons, which have no designation stamps ('Mod. 98') at all, and the Berlin-Suhler-Waffen und Fahrzeugwerke produced weapons which are marked with the BSW logo.

Between 1934 and 1945, the system of marking the receiver was changed three times. In 1934 and 1935 the marking consisted of the letter S, followed by a two or three digit-number (indicating the manufacturer) and a letter. From 1936 to early 1938, this system was continued, but with the last letter omitted. From late 1938 onward, the receiver code consisted of a two or three-digit number only. On July 1, 1940, the system was changed again. The receiver was now marked with two or three letters for the manufacturer and only two digits for the year of manufacture. Some manufacturers started only in 1941 with this method, while there are also late-war K98k's with only one digit for the year of manufacture. In 1945, the remaining, most important manufacturers were assigned new codes, consisting of three letters for the manufacturer, followed by two

digits for the year. Most of these weapons also had the model designation (Mod.98) on top of the receiver ring, instead of on the left-hand side. Finally, some K98k's feature a double manufacturers code (like ax/ar or bcd with bnz beneath), indicating that the weapons were jointly produced by two manufacturers.

| Code | Manufacturer | Year |
|---|---|---|
| S/42K | Mauser, Oberndorf | 1934 |
| S/42G | Mauser, Oberndorf | 1935 |
| S/147k | Sauer & Sohn, Suhl | 1934 |
| S/147/G | Sauer & Sohn, Suhl | 1935 |
| S/27.G | Erma, Erfurt | 1935 |
| S/243G | Mauser, Borsigwalde | 1935 |
| S/42 | Mauser, Oberndorf | 1936 - early 1938 |
| S/147 | Sauer & Sohn, Suhl | 1936 - early 1938 |
| S/27 | Erma, Erfurt | 1936 - early1938 |
| S/243 | Mauser, Borsigwalde | 1936 - early 1938 |
| S/237 | Berlin-Lübecker Maschinenfabrik, Lübeck | 1936 - early 1938 |
| BSW | Berlin-Suhler-Waffen und Fahrzeugwerke | 1937 - 1939 |
| 42 | Mauser, Oberndorf | late 1938 - 1940 |
| 147 | Sauer & Sohn, Suhl | late 1938 - 1940 |
| 27 | Erma, Erfurt | late 1938 - early 1940 |
| 243 | Mauser, Borsigwalde | late 1938 - 1940 |
| 237 | Berlin-Lübecker Maschinenfabrik, Lübeck | late 1938 - early 1940 |
| 337 | Gustloff Werke, Weimar | late 1939 - 1940 |
| 660 | Steyr-Daimler-Puch, Steyr | 1939 - early 1940 |
| ax | Feinmechanische Werke, Erfurt (formerly Erma) | late 1940 - 1941 |
| duv | Berlin-Lübecker Maschinenfabrik, Lübeck | late 1940 - 1942 |
| bnz. | Steyr-Daimler-Puch, Steyr | late 1940 - 1944 |
| **Code** | **Manufacturer** | **Year** |
| byf | Mauser, Oberndorf | 1941 - 1945 |
| byf45 | Mauser, Oberndorf | 1945 |
| svw45 | Mauser, Oberndorf | 1945 |

A selection of K98k receiver codes: see the list on the opposite and the next page.

| | | |
|---|---|---|
| CE | Sauer & Sohn, Suhl | 1941 - 1944 |
| ar | Mauser, Borsigwalde | 1941 - 1944 |
| bcd | Gustloff Werke, Weimar | 1941 - 1945 |
| ax/ar | Feinmechanische Werke & Mauser, Borsigwalde | 1941 |
| dou. | Waffen Werke Brünn, Bystrica | 1942 - 1944 |
| bcd/ar | Gustloff Werke & Mauser, Borsigwalde | 1942 - 1943 |
| dot | Waffen Werke Brünn, Brünn | 1943 - 1944 |
| bcd & bnz | Gustloff Werke & Steyr-Daimler-Puch | 1944 |
| swp45 | Waffen Werke Brünn, Brünn | 1945 |
| bnz45 | Steyr-Daimler-Puch, Steyr | 1945 |
| dou.45 | Waffen Werke Brünn, Bystrica | 1945 |

## Subcontractor codes

Many of the manufacturers listed, used parts from subcontractors to produce K98k's. The known subcontractors who delivered parts only, are listed here.

| Code | Subcontractor | Type of parts |
|---|---|---|
| a | Nahmatag, Dresden | Rear sight base and leaf |
| avk | Ruhrstal AG, Bielefeld | Barrel |
| awz | Sasse's Söhne, Vienna | Barrel |
| ayf | Erma, Erfurt | Barrel, floorplate |
| B | Carl Barth, Radeberg | Unknown |
| bpr | Grossfuss, Döbeln | Buttplate |
| brg | Schmidt Metallwarenfabrik, Döbeln | Buttplate |
| bys | Ruhrstahl AG, Witten | Barrel |
| ch | Fabrique Nationale, Herstal, Belgium | Barrel, bolt |
| crv | Fritz Werner AG, Berlin | Barrel |
| cyw | Sächsische Gußstahlwerke, Freitel | Barrel |
| d | Gebr. Bremer Maschinenfabrik, Leizpig | Unknown |
| dlv | Deutsche Edelstahlwerke AG, Remscheid | Barrel |
| dwc | Böhme & Co, Minden | Buttplate |
| e | Hermann Köhler AG, Altenburg | Trigger, bayonet mount, bolt parts |
| fxo | C.G. Haenel, Suhl | Barrel |
| gba | Adolf vom Braucke AG, Ihmerterbach bei Westig | Front sight hood |
| Geco | Gustav Genschow & Co AG, Berli | Barrel |
| ghn | Carl Ullrich & Co, Oberschonau | Bolt sleeve |
| gqm | Lock & hardenberger, Ida-Oberstein | Buttplate |
| guo | Artillerie Inrichtingen, Hembrug, Zaandam, Holland | Barrel |
| i | Elite Diamantwerk AG, Schönau/Chemnitz | Rear sight base and leaf |
| jwh | MAC, Chatellerault, France | Rear sight base, floorplate |
| K | Luck & Wagner, Suhl | Bolt stop |
| l | Astrawerke AG, Chemnitz | Receiver, bolt, bayonet mount |
| LU | Unknown | Floorplate |
| lxr | Dianawerk Mayer & Grammels pacher, Rastatt | Follower |
| m | Limbacher Maschinenfabrik, Limbach | Safety |
| n | Elsterwerder Fahrradfabrik, Elsterwerder | Bolt sleeve |
| o | Mädix Nähmaschinenteile, Dresden | Trigger, triggerguard |
| q | Julius Köhler, Limbach | Firing pin |
| qnw | Unknown | Floorplate |

Miscellaneous receiver codes. Top, from left to right: *Gewehr 98*, converted to K98k configuration, Carbine 98 ('1920' indicates this weapon belonged to the approved Reichswehr armament), *Gewehr 98*, *Standard Modell I*. Middle row: *Standard Modell II*, K98k cut-away, Portuguese crest K98k, the mysterious and probably faked 'SS-K98k' (page 19, bottom). Bottom row: Former Polish G29/40, *Luftwaffe-karabiner* (page 31, bottom), G33/40, G24(t).

# VIII PROPAGANDA PICTURES

The propaganda photos on the following pages are a special selection, depicting various aspects of the K98k in use. As mentioned before, the majority of these pictures are posed, since they were used by the Nazi regime to rig the truth. Most of the original captions are very misleading or evidently incorrect as well. Some original captions are translated and used here, but not without the necessary remarks.

In composing this selection, it was found that some subjects were far more interesting for propaganda pictures than others. The K98k sniper, for instance, was extremely popular with the photographers of the *Propaganda Kompagnie,* symbolizing the well-trained, 'lone, but determined' German soldier. Long series of photos of 'Germanic' looking types were often found as well, usually in a martial pose and with special attention for a strong chin. Other notable popular subjects were small arms cleaning, rifles with grenade launchers and scenes of day-to-day life, suggesting German soldiers were living a normal life in between the battles.

To facilitate the use of this part of the book, the pictures are classified into groups, picturing various aspects of the K98k. The subjects and pages are listed here. The pictures in the last group are, as far as possible, arranged in chronological order.

The Italian dictator, Mussolini, accompanied by some high-ranking German officers, inspects sighting exercises of an Italian soldier with a K98k. Since September 1943, when Mussolini was freed from captivity by Skorzeny and his *Fallschirmjäger* (paratroopers), he and his fascist republic in the northern part of Italy were completely dependent on German military authorities. A year after this picture was taken, Mussolini was captured by Italian partisans and subsequently executed.

Location unknown, April 27, 1944.

(Museum of Modern History, Slovenia No. 6619/11).

An army recruit tries to align the sights the proper way, while being observed by his instructor. The back sight is set on the closest range. The wooden tripod and the sand bag were standard equipment for sighting exercises and are depicted in many photographs. Note the other recruits in the background, awaiting their turn. They are all wearing brand new helmets.

France, August/September 1940.

(Bundesarchiv Koblenz, No. 59/1862/12).

Members of a Turkish volunteer unit (note the sleeve shield on the arm of the man at the left) are instructed in handling the K98k by a German NCO. This must have been basic instruction since they seem to practice the proper technique for operating the safety. The K98k on the foreground is of early manufacture, since it features a flat buttplate. The man on the right carries a bread bag. Southern Russia, Summer of 1943. (Bundesarchiv Koblenz, No. 239/2065/18a).

Shooting practice from a shooting platform. The soldier on the platform carries a gas mask in its canister, an S94/98 bayonet and a bread bag. Although his field cap is visible on the platform, it was common practice to wear the helmet during shooting practice, thus simulating the reality of warfare. The bolt on his back is probably the same camo shelter as the instructor is wearing. The soldier is operating the safety, while the instructor seems to set the back sight.
France, March 1941.
(Bundesarchiv Koblenz, No. 247/751/8).

An NCO demonstrates army recruits the loading procedure of the rifle. Both the instructor and the recruit on the left are holding a clip of *Exerzier Patrone* (dummies), consisting of a one-piece brass cartridge with a fluted case and without powder and primer. The weapons are modified *Gewehr 98s*, fitted with a new sight and a bolt assembly disc. Germany, 22 August 1940.

(SZ Photo, No.88035).

Personal shooting instruction on a well-equipped shooting range. Firing through a gap prevented the inexperienced shooter from turning his weapon to an unsafe direction. The recruit in his new uniform is carrying his cap behind his belt, but wears his helmet while firing. According to regulations, he is also carrying his gas mask, in the ribbed sheet metal canister. The K98k is of early manufacture, since it features a flat buttplate and a walnut stock.

Western Front, Autumn 1939.

(Bundesarchiv Koblenz, No. 38/311/20A).

An Airforce signal company stationed in North Africa during rifle exercises. The NCO is giving instructions, the soldiers stand to attention. Two of the K98ks are fitted with the early model muzzle/front sight cover. After the adoption of the front sight hood in december 1939, this model would no longer fit and was replaced by a simple rubber muzzle cap.
North Africa, March 1941.
(SZ Photo, No.11446).

Young army recruits cleaning their K98k's. The disassembled bolts are neatly arranged on a piece of cloth. Cleaning device model 34 is used: the oil bottle and the linked aluminum cleaning chain are clearly visible. The machined steel oiler was later replaced, first by a bakelite version and in the last year of the war by a sheet-metal oiler. Two of the three rifles have their floorplate, the spring and magazine-follower removed. The K98k's are of early production, since they feature walnut stocks and flat buttplates. Also note the early type of muzzle/front sight cover. The soldier on the right is concentrating on cleaning the front of the bolt. Western Front, Autumn 1939. (Bundesarchiv Koblenz, No. 52/1405/30).

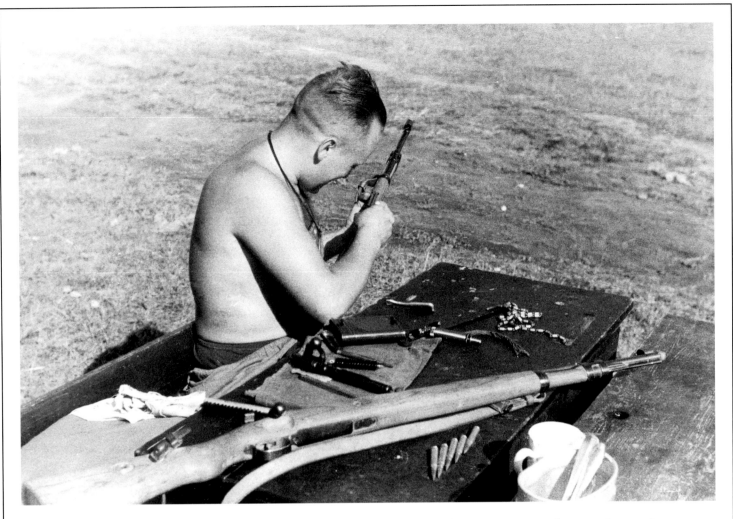

Arms cleaning in the field. The picture was taken during a battle pause at the Eastern Front. The cartridges in front, removed from the magazine during cleaning, clearly illustrate this is not an exercise. The K98k is fitted with a walnut stock, a hooded front sight and a rubber muzzle cap, a combination indicating the weapon was made in 1939. Note the cleaning device model 34 and its contents on the table. The soldier is wearing his dog tag, an oval metal disc, usually with three holes and perforations for easy breaking.

Northern Russia, September 1941.

(Bundesarchiv Koblenz, No. 212/217/19).

*Gebirgsjäger* (Mountain Troops) cleaning their weapons. Mountain Troops can be easily identified by the 'Edelweiss' (a rare mountain flower) on their field cap and upper arm. The NCO in front is holding a K98k provided with a non-hooded front sight and the early style metal muzzle cover. All K98k's in this picture, which is one of a small series, feature walnut stocks and flat buttplates.

Eastern part of France, August 1940.

(Bundesarchiv Koblenz, No. 246/709/26).

'Those who are not standing guard are cleaning their arms to keep them ready for action', states the original caption. While his men are armed with rifles, the SS officer (note the skull on his cap) with the Iron Cross in the foreground has an unidentified pistol in his hand, propably a Russian Tokarev. The rifle in the foreground features grasping grooves in the handguard, which indicates it is a *Standard Modell* or a (former) Polish G29/40.
Greece, May 1944.
(Museum of Modern History, Slovenia, No. 6615/10).

Armorers engaged in small arms field repairs. Considering the special equipment and the advanced state of disassembly, these men must be members of a specialized arms repair unit. The K98k barrel on the left even has its back sight removed, while the man on the right is studying the trigger mechanism. They are using special chests, equipped with storage places for the barrel on top and a bin underneath to collect the disassembled parts. The machine gun in the foreground is a MG34, with the barrel, receiver, mechanism and butt removed. The two men in the background are using a burner to fix another MG34.

Russia, Summer of 1942.

(Bundesarchiv Koblenz, No. 80/3162/27a).

Field repairs. An armorer has mounted a new stock on a K98k. The broken parts of the old stock are on the ground, in the left of the picture. The bolt is still missing. The chest in the background is the *Grosse Waffenmeisterkiste für MG und Handwaffen* (big armorer's chest for machine guns and small arms). The smaller chest in front, with the top tray removed, contains K98k parts. Buttplates and many other small parts are visible. For field repairs, there was also a small armorer's chest for small arms, contained in an MG cartridge box.

Russia, Summer of 1942.

(Bundesarchiv Koblenz, No. 79/3137/12).

This picture, shot in October 1941 by *PK-Kriegsberichter* Bauer, depicts the *Bezug* or carbine protector. The soldier in the centre of the picture, walking away from the photographer, is carrying a K98k on his back with this quite rare accessory. Judged to his cloths, he could very well be a *Kradfahrer* (motorcycle driver), for which this carbine protector was first adopted in 1938. Until now, this is the only photo known of this item in use.

Eastern Front, Russia, October 1941.

(SZ Photo, No.399927).

A paratrooper in his foxhole with the *Gewehrgranatgerät zur Panzerbekampfung 40* (grenade launcher for antitank use) attached to his K98k. The GG/P40 was developed especially for paratroops, since it was lighter and smaller than the standard GG42. It was manufactured and used in very small quantities only, and this is the first photo ever published of the GG/P40 in use. Note the antitank rifle grenade, which is slid over the barrel extension. Unlike the GG42, the GG/P40 was attached to the rifle with the bayonet lug. Since the safety is set on safe, this is definitely a posed picture. Location and date unknown.
(Bundesarchiv Koblenz, No. 552/823/23).

Two *Fallschirmjäger* (paratroopers) during a battle pause at the Italian front. The personal arm of the man in front is not visible, but the other carries a K98k, fitted with a grenade launcher. He also has the standard map case. According to the original caption 'The *Fallschirmjäger*, the green devils of Casino, again and again repulse the engaging masses, thus causing the heaviest losses to the enemy'. German paratroopers indeed delayed the advance of the Allies in Italy, but after a long and bitter struggle, they were finally overrun by the American and British armies. Italian front, September 13, 1944. (Museum of Modern History, Slovenia, No 6617/1).

An Estonian SS volunteer standing guard. A close study of this picture reveals an impressive amount of weapons: apart from two stick grenades, the muzzles of a K98k and a semi-automatic G41 rifle are visible. Most prominent is the K98k with grenade launcher. In the background there are some egg grenades as well. The small chest at the right of the soldier probably contains rifle grenades. For the German Army, 1944 was a year of retreat, while the Russian advance continued with ever-increasing momentum. Narva, Eastern front, March 1944. (Museum of Modern History, Slovenia, No 6618/11).

A very young German soldier poses for the photographer, near Charkov, Russia. Although young, the general appearance and the look in his eyes suggest he has already taken part in the fighting. During the course of the war, the German army was increasingly in need of personnel, since many soldiers were killed, wounded or taken prisoner, especially by the Red army. An increasing amount of foreign volunteers were recruited, but many very young and old Germans were pressed into military service as well. Generally, many young Germans were eager to serve in the army as a result of years of intense propaganda. Charkov, Summer of 1943. (Bundesarchiv Koblenz, No. 238/2018/15).

An infantryman loading the grenade launcher (*Gewehrgranat Gerät*) of his K98k. The grenade is of the explosive rifle grenade type (*Gewehr-Sprenggranate*), to be used against targets behind cover. The maximum range was about 250 meters. The explosive rifle grenade was the most common of the approximately seven types in use. Underneath the rifle the wooden chest for 20 rifle grenades is visible, containing four or five rifle grenades and some grenade cartridges (*Gewehr-Treibpatrone*). Russia, 1943.
(Bundesarchiv Koblenz, No. 89/3774/7).

The existence of this mysterious device is only known because it is depicted in some pictures; all other information is lacking. According to the original caption 'a folding, easy-to-carry tripod serves as a mounting device for firing rifle grenades from the K98k and creates a new combination of arms'. No doubt the folding tripod was inspired by a similar W.W.I device, when the German Army officially adopted two types of tripods to fire rifle grenades from the Gewehr 98. This World War II version, however, was never officially adopted and remained experimental only. Note the rifle grenade sight.
Eastern front, June 17, 1944.
(Bundesarchiv Koblenz, No. 672/7630/16).

A well-clad member of the 'Narva SS-Battalion' in winter camo, loading a rifle grenade of the *Gewehr-Panzergranate 30* (rifle antitank grenade 30) type. Note the absence of the cleaning rod, indicating the K98k is a late production type. According to the original caption, 'Machine guns, hand grenades and rifle grenades awaiting the advancing Soviets. The men of the Narva Battalion have rejected several attacks of the Soviet army during the previous days, thus preventing the intended breakthrough.'
Eastern front, January, 1944.
(Museum of Modern History, Slovenia, No. 6489/12).

This picture is one of a series with small mutual differences and is a classical example of a propaganda picture. The soldier with a grenade launcher attached to his rifle, leaving his underground shelter, had to repeat this scene over and over again, until the photographer was satisfied with the result. It took many pictures before the desired warlike expression on his face had met expectations. Also note the scarce camouflage attached to the helmet: this was only useful for producing better pictures. Eastern Front, June 1943. (Bundesarchiv Koblenz, No. 219/566/3a).

A volunteer from northwestern Europe, serving in the *Waffen-SS*, during fights for a Russian village. His K98k rifle is fitted with a grenade launcher. On the background a burning farm or barn.

Eastern Front, Russia, July 1942.

(SZ Photo, No.71833).

A technically poor, but nevertheless very powerful (and posed) picture. According to the original caption 'The men have regrouped themselves and the attack is launched. Behind the protective armored cars, which will have to bear the main burden of Soviet anti-tank fire, the tanks follow with the grenadiers on them'. The bayonet is fixed to the rifle, probably at the request of the photographer. The grenadier is also carrying a leather pouch containing the rifle grenade launcher.
Eastern front, 18 May, 1944.
(Museum of Modern History Slovenia, No. 6617/3).

'The grenadiers of the infantery regiment *Grossdeutschland*, in which volunteers from all parts of Germany are serving, receive a stringent infantry training before they are sent to battle. An exercise on the surprise training ground. The soldier runs, fires at unexpectedly appearing enemies, and finally stabs the suddenly arising dummy with his bayonet. His rush is escorted by the instructor', reads the original caption of this picture of *Kriegsberichter* Fremke. Germany, April 1942. (SZ Photo, No.319973).

A German infantry soldier during assault training in the Eiffel mountains, with his rifle with fixed bayonet in his right hand and his scoop in his left hand. This picture was shot shortly before the start of the Campaign in the West, in which the German army overran Belgium, the Netherlands, Luxembourg and France in only six weeks of time.
Eiffel, Germany, April 1940.
(SZ Photo, No.67626).

Fuseliers of the Grossdeutschland-division in house-to-house figthing. Considering the gloves and position of the right hand of the man on the left, his K98k is fitted with a winter trigger. His companion is armed with a pistol, probably an FN-Browning High Power.

Although it is often reported that the winter trigger was quite common, it is seldom seen in pictures. The winter trigger arrangement (*Winterabzug*) was developed in 1942, but only officially adopted in 1944. It consisted of an oval sheet metal box with a lever inside. By pulling an external button backwards, the internal lever depressed the trigger.

Location unknown, March 10, 1944. (Museum of Modern History, Slovenia, No. 6619/6).

'The High School of Artillery. Small caliber shooting at the artillery. For efficiency reasons, the first firing exercises are not carried out with real cannon, but with a special device that combines the standard sights of a cannon with a small calibre gun', reads the official caption.

The picture depicts four of these sighting devices, each fitted with a K98k receiver with bolt and trigger mechanism and a shortened barrel. Obviously, this method of training was far cheaper than live firing exercises with a large caliber gun.

Germany, 17 April 1940.

(SZ Photo, No.381946).

Sighting instruction with the *Zielkontrollspiegel* (target mirror). The target mirror is mounted between the rear sight and the receiver by means of a clamp. The shooter is aiming his rifle, while the instructor is looking in the mirror to observe his operations. These mirrors were also used on the *Klein-Kaliber-Wehrsportgewehr* or KKW (small caliber military and sporting rifle). Note the spent cases and the (empty) cartridge boxes beneath the rifle.

France, 1941.

(Bundesarchiv Koblenz, No. 227/266/20)

This unique series of photographs depicts the very rare indirect fire device for rifles. It is reported that this device was designated *Deckungszielgerät*. It was developed late 1942 or early 1943, when the German advance in Russia was brought to a standstill. The trench warfare in certain sectors of this front led to the re-introduction of some World War I devices, among which this indirect fire device for rifles. During the Great War, a similar device was used for the Gewehr 98. However, while in World War I the indirect fire device for rifles was rather common, in the Second World War it remained a very rare item.

Russia, Charkov, June 1943.

(Bundesarchiv Koblenz, No. 238/2014/21)

The purpose of the indirect firing device is being demonstrated: the K98k is being fired, while the shooter remains behind his cover. The shooter looks through the periscopic sight, while his left hand pulls the chain, which is attached to the trigger. The device was designed to be used with the K98k, the G43 and K43 and other rifles and carbines with similar butt stocks. It also accepted the Russian Tokarev semi-automatic rifle, which indicates these weapons were widely used.

Russia, Charkov, June 1943.

(Bundesarchiv Koblenz,

No. 238/2014/20)

A detailed view, clearly showing the main parts of the indirect firing device for rifles. The rifle butt was inserted into the housing and secured by the top clamps. Then the lever (on the right side) was turned to tighten the cam against the stock, and all butterfly nuts and set screws were tightened. The trigger hook was hooked behind the trigger and the chain was tensed by snapping the snaphook into one of the chain links. Finally, the periscope was clamped on and adjusted.
Russia, Charkov, June 1943.
(Bundesarchiv Koblenz, No. 238/2014/22)

Back side view, showing the periscopic sight. It is obvious that the indirect firing device was only suited for static defense because it was heavy (weight 5.6 kg) and bulky. And since the stalemate conditions of the Great War were seldom encountered in World War II, the device saw only very limited use. Actually, these pictures depict the only known example of a W.W.II version. It is not known if a specimen still exists. Russia, Charkov, June 1943. (Bundesarchiv Koblenz, No. 238/2014/19)

This is probably the most mysterious propaganda picture in this book. The K98k, demonstrated to the photographer, is obviously converted to fire flare cartridges. The barrel is removed and the front part of the receiver ring is cut off. In front of the receiver ring a new part is installed, probably to grasp behind the rim of the bottom of the flare cartridge. Finally, the inside of the front part of the stock is clad with sheet metal or aluminum.

To fire a flare cartridge from this device without a proper top cover, however, is a dangerous job; the case itself is not strong enough to withstand the gas pressure. There are two possible solutions to this mystery. Either a sort of top cover is used but is just not shown, or this is a dangerous experiment by a local armorer or the resistance.

Russia, 1943/1944.

(Bundesarchiv Koblenz, No. 241/2193/29A)

*Fallschirmjäger* (paratroopers) in a training center practicing jumping techniques with K98k 'mock-ups'. This is one of a series of pictures, in which several wooden K98k-like rifles are depicted. Although no information on these 'weapons' was found, it seems logical not to use 'live' K98k's in training courses like these. A close study of this picture reveals that these mock-ups were not just unfinished stocks but purposely made. Note the ring-shaped cut out part in the butt, probably to attach an improvised sling on the other side of the 'rifle'.

Location and date unknown.

(Bundesarchiv Koblenz, No. 547/683/33)

'At the Sovjet-front. The circle is closing. A reconaissance unit goes forward to asses the effects of the German artillery', according to the official caption of this picture of *SS-PK Kriegsberichter* Roth. The members of this *SS* unit are armed with K98k's, one of the rifles fitted with a grenade launcher, and an MG34. The machinegun is not visible, but the third man from the left carries a spare barrel container and a 300-rd ammo drum for this weapon.

Eastern Front, Russia, July 1941.

(SZ Photo, No.383352).

An SS sniper and his spotter, clad in the distinctive dapple-pattern camouflage, are observing the enemy lines in a foxhole near a cornfield. The K98k is cocked and the bolt-safety is in the on position. The telescopic sight is a commercial *Zielvier* or military contract ZF39-type, mounted on a turret mount. The soldier on the left is armed with a Beretta model 38/44 submachine gun, which was widely used by the German army, especially in the last phase of the war. Between both men, the rear end of a *Panzerfaust* is visible.

Eastern front, Siebenbürgen, October 30, 1944.

(Museum of Modern History, Slovenia).

Two pictures of a Mountain Troops sniper in the Alps. His K98k is fitted with a fourfold magnification telescopic sight mounted on a turret mount. On his cap is the Mountain Troops' white metal badge in the form of the Edelweiss flower. The original caption says 'This man from East-Tirol is a son of the mountains. No movement will escape his trained eyes. Every spotted target will be hit'. Actually, this was a posed picture and one of a small series.

Western part of the Alps, January, 1945.

(Museum of Modern History, Slovenia, No. 6615/12).

This is the same Mountain Troops sniper as in the previous picture, now seen from behind and with his hood pulled on. According to the original caption 'These high positions are closing off the entire valley. Snipers and machine guns prevent the enemy from advancing.' Since the photographer belonged to an SS propaganda unit, this sniper was probably a member of the SS Mountain Troops.

Western part of the Alps, January, 1945.

(Museum of Modern History, Slovenia, No. 6489/10).

A well-camouflaged sniper looking for targets. Note the fur and cloth wrapped around the front part of the stock and barrel, probably both for camouflage and to prevent damage to the stock. The telescopic sight with fourfold magnification is mounted on a turret mount. Apart from the 1.5-fold ZF41, this is the most common K98k sniper configuration. Although the snow and uniform suggest very cold conditions, the sniper has neither gloves nor a winter trigger.

Norway, December 1943.

(Bundesarchiv Koblenz, No. 106/1266/22).

A sniper carrying a K98k with a fourfold magnification telescopic sight mounted on a short side rail mount. The original caption states 'In the strong defense lines near Sebastopol, the German grenadier is prepared to fight the far more numerous masses of the Soviets. A sniper is going to take position in the foremost trenches'.

Note the World War I like trenches and the worn-out uniform. With a grueling winter behind it, the German Army in Russia now faced a massive attack by the Red Army and a long retreat to the west. Sebastopol, Eastern front, April 28, 1944.

(Museum of Modern History, Slovenia, No. 6489/6).

Two experienced front soldiers, a sniper and his spotter, looking for targets. The spotter is wearing a close combat clasp and the Crimea sleeve shield. The K98k sniper rifle is fitted with a short side rail mounted telescopic sight.

According to the original caption 'a warm welcome is prepared here for the Soviets'. However, within two weeks after this picture was made, Sebastopol was liberated by the Soviet army and over 30,000 Germans were taken prisoner. The photographer was the same who took the previous picture.

Sebastopol, Eastern front, April 29, 1944.

(Museum of Modern History, Slovenia, No. 6619/12).

A sniper looking for a target under cover behind a thick board wall. The telescopic sight is mounted on a turret mount. Note the lens covers attached to the sight. This is a posed picture and one of a small series.

The grenadier is wearing the reversible winter uniform: white for use in snow on one side and multicolored in greens and browns on the reverse side. It was devised after the disastrous winter of 1941-1942, when many members of the unprepared German army literally froze to death.

Russia, June 12, 1944.

(Bundesarchiv Koblenz, No. 90/3939/29).

This is one of a small series of photographs, which seem not to have been posed. A squad of riflemen in the platform of a military truck has probably spotted the enemy, although there seems to be no imminent threat. The man in the center is manipulating the safety of his K98k, while most others are concentrated on events out of sight. The man on the right carries a K98k sniper rifle, but he shows no intention to sight his rifle. The sniper rifle is fitted with a ZF39 telecopic sight, mounted on a low turret mount.

Northern Russia, Summer of 1941.

(Bundesarchiv Koblenz, No. 208/21/28).

'The optical eye sees everything ... and the sniper behind it knows how to aim', the original caption states. The front view of a sniper was a popular subject for propaganda pictures and it is safe to assume these were always posed. As in many similar situations, the marksman has camouflaged his helmet with his hood. The left half of his face is covered with a kind of veil as well. The telescopic sight is mounted on a turret mount, but other details are not visible.
Location unknown, May 16, 1944. (Museum of Modern History, Slovenia No. 6619/5).

95

Camouflaging the K98k. Such elaborate camouflage of the weapon is seldom seen. To hide the rifle, usually strips of cloth were used which wrapped the length of the weapon. The helmet is covered by the hood jacket, while a string around the snipers leg is used to attach grass. Also note the string to tighten the sleeve around the right wrist. This is to prevent the sleeve from catching on protruding parts of the weapon. The K98k is of later manufacture, since it features a cupped buttplate and a hooded frontsight. The telescopic sight is nearly invisible. Location unknown, July 7, 1944. (Museum of Modern History, Slovenia, No. 6574a/4).

'The sniper enters a cornfield. With his camouflage adapted to the surroundings he is nearly invisible', the original caption states. The art of camouflage was an important part of basic sniper training. Apart from standard equipment, there was an endless variety of improvised camouflage outfits.

As in most other sniper pictures, this marksman has camouflaged the distinct silhouette of his helmet. The net, covering his face, seems to be a bit superfluous. The lens covers of the turret mounted telecopic sight are visible.

Location unknown, July 7, 1944. (Museum of Modern History, Slovenia, No. 6604/5).

Two German *Fallschirmjäger* have captured a British soldier. The man on the left holds an early issue K98k with a turret mounted telescopic sight, while the other is armed with a MP 38 submachine gun. Note the cloth bandoleers, carried by the *Falschirmjäger* on the right, which contain 100 rounds of ammunition.

Although the original caption is missing, this picture was obviously taken during the German invasion of Crete. This island was occupied by German *Fallschirmjäger* in May 1941, but only after fights with took such a heavy toll on German paratroopers that they were never deployed in large-scale parachute operations again.

Crete, May 1941.

(Bundesarchiv Koblenz, No. 166/509/36).

'The pine boughs at the edge of the trench and the camouflage smock make the sniper practically invisible. Often, he has to wait patiently for a long time, before he finds a target', the original caption states. The K98k sniper rifle features a military contract telescopic sight mounted on a turret mount. It is provided with a flattened safety as well, which is in the off position. This propaganda photograph was taken at the Lauer river, in eastern Germany, at the beginning of the last winter of World War II.

The Lauer river, Germany, November 24, 1944.

(Museum of Modern History, Slovenia, No. 6619/9).

A marksman is checking his ZF41 telescopic sight after leaving his shelter. Although the weather conditions seems to require a winter trigger arrangment, the rifle has no such device. The man is carrying binoculars and a three-section MP 38/40 magazine pouch as well. Although the 1.5 magnification ZF41 was optically deficient for effective sniping, and the K98k-ZF 41 assembly was even officially downgraded to an ordinary *Karabiner* in early 1944, production and issue continued until the very last weeks of the war.

Norway, 1943.

(Bundesarchiv Koblenz, No. 100/795/25).

A K98k sniper with a ZF41 (*Zielfernrohr 41*) telescopic sight at the Dniepr river in a posed picture. According to the German caption, 'Our snipers are increasingly successful. Reports of 40, 50 or 60 hits in a short timespan are not rare. They are often very useful in eliminating forward enemy scouts.' In reality, the German army was fighting a lost battle against a heavy Soviet attack in that region. In the fall and winter of 1943, the Red Army crossed the Dniepr over a great length and forced the Germans to a 'tactical' retreat. Dniepr river, Eastern front, May 19, 1944.
(Museum of Modern History, Slovenia, No. 6615/8).

German soldiers climbing a mountain. According to the original caption, these grenadiers are carrying ammunition and supplies to their comrades. Their defense lines near the Mediterranean are being shelled by American warships, supporting their advancing infantry.

The rifle of the foremost soldier - who is obviously not enjoying the trip - is a Czech Vz24, featuring a straight bolt handle, bottom mounted sling swivels and a full handguard with fingergrooves. The collar tab on the soldier's left upper sleeve indicates he is a member of a signal unit. Southern France, Provence region, 1944.

(Museum of Modern History, Slovenia, No. 6621/4).

Members of the guard on the *Panzerschiff Admiral Scheer* present their rifles, during the ceremony of the official adoption of this vessel on 12 November 1934. The weapons are *Gewehr* 98 transitional model rifles, typical for the Weimar Republic. These guns were usually made from WWI rifles, by replacing the original backsight with a simple tangent rear side and the marking disc in the buttstock by a bolt disassembly disc. However, the rifles on this picture also feature grasping grooves in the stock, typical for the World War I *Radfahrer Gewehr* (Bicyclists' Rifle) and its successor, the K98b Carbine. But contrary to these two types, the weapons of the guard on the *Admiral Scheer* are fitted with a parade hook to the upper band for sling shortening and a swivel to the rear of the pistol grip stock wrist. Wilhemshaven, Germany, 12 November 1934.
(SZ Photo, No.380496).

A railway lorry manned by two German soldiers and a *Gefreiter* (corporal), armed with K98k rifles. Such lorries were used to guard railway lines against sabotage and raids by partisans, which continued to remain a serious problem for the German troops in Russia.

Russia, Date unknown.

(SZ Photo, No.381744).

Very peaceful use of two bayonet-mounted K98k rifles in North Afrika. Two members of the *Afrikakorps* have employed their weapons as tent poles, to create some shadow in the blistering heat of the desert.
North Africa, March 1942.
(SZ Photo, No.87614).

German soldiers crossing a destroyed bridge, blown-up by the Soviet army to delay the advance of the enemy. This picture was shot on 22 June 1941, the first day of the invasion and the beginning of the end of the Third Reich. The soldiers carry their rifles on the back, which indicates there is no imminent danger.

Western Russia, 22 June 1941.

(SZ Photo, No.10448).

Bosnian volunteers in the *Waffen-SS*, very probably members of the 13. *SS-Freiwilligen Gebirgs Division 'Handschar'*, during exercises. The nickname 'Handschar' comes from the Arabian sword with the curved blade, which was also depicted on the right collar patch. This unit was mainly deployed on the Balkan to fight communist partisans and became notorious for its cruelty.

Germany, 20 December 1943.

(SZ Photo, No.6513).

This picture depicts a ceremony in which army recruits receive their weapon immediate after they have taking the oath. Himmler had ordered that the ceremony had to express the unity of the home front and the fighting army. The officer therefore takes the K98ks from the arms of a labourer of the arms industry. This picture was shot in 1945 and the late-production type K98k that is handed over is fitted with a sheet-metal top band, but still features a bolt disassembly disc.

Germany, 1945.

(SZ Photo, No.95662).

A very strong propaganda photo, depicting three grenadiers of the *Waffen-SS* awaiting the order for the assault, according to the original caption. This picture was extensively retouched: the helmets of the men in the centre and on the right have been made darker, and the earth wall on the background to the right was completely added, probably to hide a disturbing detail.
Eastern Front, Russia, 1943.
(SZ Photo, No.67624).

According to the caption, this picture depicts an NCO inspects the K98k rifle of a 17-year old recruit in military barracks, but the boy and the other recruit at the background are probably younger. All three rifles on this picture feauture the early model muzzle/front sight cover.
Germany, 1944.
(SZ Photo, No.35609).

A technically poor but impressive propaganda photo shot by *PK* Styhler. The caption reads 'A stick grenade will break the last resistance.' An assault unit of the *SS* in close combat with Sovjet troops.
Eastern Front, Russia, Summer 1941.
(SZ Photo, No.38397).

'At the Sovjetfront. Battery after battery is being destroyed by the *Sturmgeschützen* (assault guns). The gun crews are on the run and offer our infantry good targets. They open fire from behind the protection of the steel giants', reads the official caption of *PK-Kriegsberichter* Lessmann.

Either this caption does not tell the truth, or Lessmann was a very brave photographer: while the infantrymen are firing from behind an assault gun, the photo was shot from an exposed position.

Eastern Front, Seljonowo, Russia, August 1941.

(SZ Photo, No.319767).

An infantry-unit in a trench, according to the official caption awaiting the order to assault. The *Obergefreiter* on the foreground holds a K98k rifle with a *Gewehrgranatgerät* 42, and with his left hand he is manipulating the grenade launcher sight. The soldier in the centre is armed with an MG34 machinegun. This picture was shot near lake Ilmen, located in northwest Russia between Moscow and St.Petersburg. About 100.000 German soldiers remained encircled in this region for nearly a year, before they finally managed to break through the siege.
Lake Ilmen, Russia, unknown date. (SZ Photo, No.398328).

A German infanterist aims his K98k rifle, fitted with the bayonet, at Russian troops. This picture was shot in a wood near Mogilev (Russia), only some weeks after the start of the German attack on Russia.

Eastern Front, Mogilev, Russia, July 1941.

(SZ Photo, No.78521).

A young German soldier in a shelter prepares a *Panzerfaust* 100. Behind him, a K98k with grenade launcher is against the parapet. This picture was shot at the Oder river in northern Germany, about four weeks before the capitulation of the German army.

Oder river, Germany, 9 April 1945.

(SZ Photo, No.52668).

'In the dense forests of the Vosges region, our well-hidden and camouflaged grenadiers wait in their foxholes to repel Anglo-American attacks', the German caption states. The man on the left is armed with a K98k, while his comrade has a Czech Vz24 (*Gewehr* 24(t)). Note the straight bolt handle, the long hand guard and the design of the lower band. For camouflage, both men use their shelter triangle with splinter pattern. Vosges region, western Germany, November 17, 1944. (Museum of Modern History, Slovenia, No. 6215).

A surrealistic picture of German soldiers trying to clear something from snow with three rifles on the foreground. Apparently, the rifles are no K98k's; they all feature a full handguard, protruding behind the back sight. The weapons on the left and on the right of the picture have a bent down bolt handle and a sling swivel on the right side of the stock, near the pistol grip. The rifle in the middle features a straight bolt handle, while the sling seems to be attached to the buttstock in the 'normal' way. Also note the sight ears to protect the front sight. It is believed the rifle in the middle is a (former) Polish Wz29/40, while both other weapons are variations of the Czech Vz24 rifle.

Russia, 1941.

(Bundesarchiv Koblenz, No. 215/351/4).

During the very last months of the war, members of the Schleswig *Volkssturm* have prepared a defense line. They are awaiting the advancing Red Army at the borders of the Oder river, where the western and eastern allies would meet at the end of the war.

Apart from the MG34 with its receiver cover, the soldiers are armed with World War I *Gewehr 98*'s in their original configuration: note the distinctive backsight for the W.W.I 'S'-ammunition. Also note the G98's straight bolt handle and the short hand guard.

The Oder river, northern Germany, February 13, 1945.

(Museum of Modern History, Slovenia, No. 5993/6).

Stacked *Gewehr 98*'s in front of destroyed buildings, somewhere in Northern Russia. Note the grasping grooves, the straight bolt handles and the position of the sling swivels. Although many G98's were shortened and converted to K98k configuration, some propaganda photos depict unshorted rifles. The rifles in this picture are converted to the sS-cartridge, since they feature the new back sight. They are fitted with a bolt disassembly disc as well.

Northern Russia, August/September 1941.

(Bundesarchiv Koblenz, No. 211/172/17).

A K98k with its predecessor, a K98a. Although both weapons feature many similarities, the differences are easy to spot. Note the K98a's protected front sight, the stacking hook and the long handguard. The sling swivels are mounted at the underside, which is unusual: most K98a feature a side-mounted sling.

The text on the canister reads *Waffenentfettungsmittel* (degreasing fluid), indicating the well-protected man in the photo is engaged in preparing stored weapons for use.

Russia, June/July 1941.

(Bundesarchiv Koblenz, No. 137/1040/31a).

Six K98k rifles are stacked during a lunch break. All rifles are of early manufacture, in perfect condition and fitted with the early style metal muzzle protectors, which is logical, as this picture was taken in 1939.

The man left of the rifles is wearing his oval identification disc over his shirt. Also note the boots' soles with the characteristic hobnails. To mark the difference, the officer's boots (on the left) are provided with toe plates as well. Western front, 1939.

(Bundesarchiv Koblenz, No. 42/618/33).

Loading the K98k magazine with the stripper clip. To load the rifle, the bolt is opened and the loaded clip inserted to the clip-charger guideway slot in the receiver bridge. Then the cartridges are pushed down by the thumb into the magazine. The mainspring of bolt is automatically cocked and the empty clip falls away when the bolt is closed.

Note the K98k's hooded front sight and the cupped buttplate. The belt buckle with the text '*Gott mit uns*' is clearly visible, as are some ammunition pouches.

Location and date unknown.

(Bundesarchiv Koblenz, No. 206/1865/17).

A Pak 38 with its crew, consisting of five men: a leader, a gunner, a loader and two ammunition carriers. The Pak 38 (*Panzerabwehrkanone Modell 1938*: anti-tank gun Model 1938) was introduced in 1938, but it took three years before a substantial amount was available. In the early years of the war the 50 mm shell was still effective. Later on, when more heavily armored allied tanks appeared, its performance became inadequate. By then, the 88 mm FLAK (*Flugzeugabwehrkanone*: anti-aircaft gun) was increasingly and successfully employed against enemy tanks and armored cars. The K98k in the foreground is cocked and in the fire position.

France, 1941.

(Bundesarchiv Koblenz, No. 251/968/28).

Firepower. A rack with K98k rifles in front of a railway cannon. The gun is a 28 cm *Kurze Bruno* (short Bruno) on a 'Vögele' turn table. Krupp delivered 12 to 15 of these railway cannons to the German army. *Kurze Bruno* had a weight of 130,000 kg and featured a 11 meter barrel. The projectile had a weight of 240 kg and a maximum range of 30 km. In the photograph, a shell is being unloaded from a tackle. The crew members have put their personal weapons in an arms rack, an item that did not add much weight to the cannon.

France, Summer of 1941.

(Bundesarchiv Koblenz, No. 224/35/17a).

A detailed view of the rifle rack containing eighteen K98k's. By 1941, fighting in France had long ceased, thus the K98k's are in excellent condition and they are all of early manufacture. The weapons feature walnut stocks with flat buttplates and are fitted with the early style muzzle caps. In the background, the crew is engaged in elevating the barrel, by means of gigantic cranks on both sides of the gun.

France, Summer of 1941.

(Bundesarchiv Koblenz, No. 224/35/18a).

A marksman sighting his rifle from the inside of a house. This picture is very likely to be posed, as the conditions are too well balanced: without the small amount of light from the left, the soldier would become nearly invisible. Note the way the soldier is using his left hand to provide more stability.

Northern Russia, Summer of 1941.

(Bundesarchiv Koblenz, No. 208/9/7).

A squad of riflemen on the platform of a truck ready to open fire. It is difficult to say whether this scene was posed, or if the situation was actually threatening. Note the K98k on the left is cocked and the safety is in the fire position. The man in the middle operates an MG34 machine gun, of which the fixed mount is visible in the foreground. Note the textured surface of the helmets - to prevent dangerous glittering - and the straps for attaching foliage.

Russia, June 1941.

(Bundesarchiv Koblenz, No. 209/58/12).

A still life with K98k's and individual equipment. The two nearly brand-new sets of personal equipment suggest some recruits have undressed themselves, probably to take a bath in a river. Note the condition of the backpacks with ponyfur, the leather belts and the cartridge pouches: they seem to have been issued only shortly before. The gray woolen socks are of regular issue, with white rings to indicate their size. Both K98k's are fitted with walnut stocks, flat buttplates and the early style metal muzzle cap.
France, August 1941.
(Bundesarchiv Koblenz,
No. 228/308/16a).

A company during a ceremony, probably to decorate the man with the flowers in the left of the picture. The man in front of him holds a tray with a bottle, a mess canteen and a small box, which could contain a decoration. The commander of the company is visible at the left. Note the peculiar way in which the slings of the stacked K98k's are tightened. This was probably done to prevent them from touching the ground without shortening the slings with the buckle. The walnut stocked K98k's are in very good condition and are fitted with rubber muzzle caps, introduced in 1939. Northern Russia, September 1941. (Bundesarchiv Koblenz, No. 212/230/12a).

Heavily armed infantry shock troops engaging the enemy with K98k rifles and a MG34 machine gun. A second MG34 gunner is waiting, probably to relieve the first one when he has to change barrels or to load a new belt of ammunition. Note the flamethrower in the background, a very fearful weapon against which there was nearly no cover or protection. Flammable oil was pressed out by nitrogen, ignited at the mouth of the nozzle and then produced a jet of flame. Since the maximum range was 20 to 25 meters, succesfull action was only possible at a short distance and with surprise; no doubt, any enemy would first try to eliminate a flamethrower before turning to any other weapon or menace.

Northern Russia, September 1941.

(Bundesarchiv Koblenz, No. 212/203/31).

A column of grenadiers advancing under cover of a *Panzerkampfwagen III*, somewhere in Russia. Apart from the two K98k's, a MG34 machine gun and many of its accessories are visible. The man on the right carries a container with a spare barrel, while the man on the left has a belt box. The man in front of him carries the tripod. The soldier standing at the right has a belt box as well, and he is armed with a Russian PPSh submachine gun.

Russia, October 1941.

(Bundesarchiv Koblenz, No. 213/278/18).

Army recruits during exercises. They have to assist each other while climbing over the wooden fence wearing their basic equipment. This consisted (from top to bottom) of a messkit, a shelter triangle (*Zeltbahn*), a ribbed canister with gasmask and a canteen with cup. The shelter triangle was used for rain protection and camouflage, while four triangles could be buttoned together to make a tent for four men. The soldiers also carry the Y-straps, a belt with a S94/98 bayonet and ammunition pouches for the K98k. All visible rifles are K98k's of early manufacture. France, December 1941. (Bundesarchiv Koblenz, No. 253/1058/18a).

Definitely not an arranged or posed picture and therefore a rather rare example. These three men obviously return from a very recent fight, in which the officer in the middle has been wounded on his right hand or arm. Note the blood stains over the uniforms and the very agitated look in their eyes. They don't seem to like being photographed at this very moment. The men to the side are armed with K98k's with walnut stocks and flat buttplates, while the officer is carrying an MP38 submachine gun on his shoulder.

Location unknown, 1941.

(Bundesarchiv Koblenz, No. 226/178/26a).

Under enemy fire. Very probably not a posed picture. The position of the photographer is unusually low, while the look in the eyes of both soldiers is not martial, but expresses fear. They seem to have no intention whatsoever to look over the edge of their trench. In the foreground the boots of a killed or wounded soldier are visible.

The K98k of the man in the middle, with a cupped buttplate and a hooded front, is cocked. In front of him is a container for mortar grenades.

Russia, March 1943.

(Bundesarchiv Koblenz, No. 237/1091/8).

The company barber at work in the field. Scenes like these were very popular for propaganda pictures, emphasizing 'the normal life' enlisted soldiers were living in the army. The photographer tried to make the picture more interesting by arranging all kinds of equipment over the barber's table, including a K98k of early manufacture, a field cap, a folding spade and a bayonet SG94/98 (*Seitengewehr 94/98*) for the K98k. Also note the tent in the background. Russia, June 1943. (Bundesarchiv Koblenz, No. 219/585/22).

'Eastern Prussia. Characteristic for the frontline are the big lakes and the surrounding woods. Our main defense line consists of strengthened trenches on the western side of the lake. Sentries are constantly watching the other side, which is controlled by the Soviets. More than once, nightly crossings of the enemy were repulsed bloody with heavy and light arms', according to the German caption. Note the muzzle of the K98k, which is fitted with an irregular muzzle protector and attached by means of a small chain.
Eastern Prussia, October 20, 1944. (Museum of Modern History, Slovenia, No. 6624/1).

'On his post in a foxhole. The fur-lined winter anorak with a hood, that is also lined with fur, protects the SS-Panzer grenadier from the cold. Winter boots with felt are keeping the feet warm', the original German caption states. In the winter of 1942-1943, when this picture was taken, the German army had learned the costly lessons from the previous winter, when there were virtually no winter uniforms. To stress the difference, many pictures were taken with soldiers in warm and fur-lined uniforms.

In the foreground is one of the first Panzerfausts: these weapons were only introduced in the summer of 1943. The K98k, cocked and in the safe position, features a front sight hood but has no cleaning rod. Eastern front, December 10, 1943. (Museum of Modern History, Slovenia, No. 6605/14).

'The crew of a heavy anti-aircraft cannon, which closes off an important supply route of Soviet tank assaults, is trying to stay warm' the original caption states. As mentioned before, the 88 mm FLAK was often deployed as an anti-tank gun when more heavily armored allied, especially Russian T34, tanks appeared.

The soldier on the right is probably returning from guard duties. He is carrying a cocked and locked K98k, together with the basic equipment: bayonet, folding shovel, mess kit, gas mask in canister and canteen.

Eastern front, February 12, 1944.

(Museum of Modern History, Slovenia, No. 6616/16).

'The noise of tracks! The SS-Panzer-grenadier is looking through his binoculars to find out if enemy tanks are approaching. Apart from his rifle, he holds a *Panzerfaust*', the caption states. This pose, a heavily armed soldier with a resolute chin concentrated on an important job, was one of the propaganda photographer's favorites.

The *Panzerfaust* is of the type 30. The flat metal strip on the launch tube is the sight, the small tube beneath contains the mechanism to cock and fire the weapon, which could penetrate 200 mm armored plate at a maximum range of 30 meters. Also note the flare pistol, a Walther Model 1934 type.

Eastern front, July 1944.

(Museum of Modern History, Slovenia, No. 5886/11).

A World War I-like scene. One man is observing the enemy lines with a trench periscope, while the other is sighting his rifle. Although not visible, the rifle may be fitted with a ZF 41 telescopic sight. This picture is very probably a posed one, but they have at least taken the trouble to cock the K98k and to set the safety to the off position.
Southern Russia, 1944.
(Bundesarchiv Koblenz, No. 241/2192/13).

Pseudo-Germanic ideology was a proven part of Nazi propaganda. Especially Himmler, head of the SS, was engaged in developing a sort of religion. These three men are reading the text on a freshly mounted route sign. The text reads *Burgenhöhe Helgoland*, *Nibelungenhang* and *Wolfsschlucht*, meaning respectively 'Castle hill Helgoland', 'Hazy hill' (actually an untranslatable notion from Wagner's operas) and 'The Wolf's Gorge'.

Although this picture was taken in the last phase of the war, the man in the front of the photograph is carrying an early manufacture K98k with a walnut stock and a flat buttplate. Note that the bolt is cocked and the safety is in the on position. Eastern Front, July 1944.
(Bundesarchiv Koblenz, No. 243/2255/14).

Sappers are cutting holes in the ice beneath the snow. According to the original German caption, the icefield is being mined, to prevent the Soviet army from crossing this area with heavy material.

Both men have put their K98k's in the snow in the only correct way: with the butts down. Note the hooded front sight of the rifle in the foreground and the belt with ammunition pouches and the bayonet beneath.

Eastern front, Narva region, April 11, 1944.

(Museum of Modern History, Slovenia, No. 3333).

'Fresh troops from the *Heimat* marching to the front', according to the original German caption. However, considering their age, their self-confident look and the captured Russian PPSh41 submachine gun, these are experienced soldiers and by no means 'fresh troops from the *Heimat*'. Note the canister on the left, containing a spare barrel for a MG34 or MG42 machine gun, the cartridge belt and the egg and stick grenade. Location unknown, August 22, 1944. (Museum of Modern History, Slovenia, No. 6490/15).

'Paratroopers at the western front. Paratrooper sentries on an mined bridge overlooking the terrain', according to the German caption. Although one should expect the *Fallschirmjäger*, as an elite unit, to be armed with automatic or semi-automatic weapons such as the G43 rifle or the Sturmgewehr, most pictures show them with ordinary K98k rifles. Both K98k's on this picture are of late production. They feature cupped buttplates, no cleaning rods and the late type upper band configuration. Also note the egg grenades.

France, September 9, 1944.

(Museum of Modern History, Slovenia No 6616/14).

'In the center of the eastern front. These days, the snow has covered the frozen earth. In the third winter of the war, the trench guards have covered their warm uniforms with the white camouflage jackets again', according to the original caption. This is not correct, since the soldiers wear the reversible winter jacket, with white for use in snow on one side and multicolored in greens and browns on the reverse side.

The K98k features a cupped buttplate, a sheet metal upper band and no cleaning rod. Note the setting of the back sight, which indicates the shooter is aiming at a long range target. Combined with the spotter with binoculars, this looks like a sniper team without a scoped rifle.

Eastern front, November 1944.

(Museum of Modern History, Slovenia, No. 6603/20).

'The front line in Latvia. The commander of an infantry division in the foremost observation post', the original caption states. Note the small pile of ammunition boxes to the left of the K98k, with a filled stripper clip on top. Each box contains 15 rounds in three stripper clips.

A German infantry division had an official strength of 16,860 men, consisting of 518 officers, 102 administrators, 2573 non-commissioned officers and 13,667 men. The main small arm was the K98k, of which an infantry division had 12,609 pieces in its inventory. During W.W.II, there were 249 infantry divisions in the German army.

Latvia, Eastern front, October 6, 1944.

(Museum of Modern History, Slovenia, No. 6624/3).

According to the original German caption 'Danish SS volunteers have recaptured a hill, which was occupied by the Red Army the night before. Now a flare cartridge is fired, to indicate the positions of the advanced infantry to their own artillery'.

Apart from the Walther Model 1934 flare pistol, the man is carrying a late production K98k with a laminated stock, a sheet-metal upper band and no cleaning rod.

Eastern front, Libau region, October 1944.

(Museum of Modern History, Slovenia, No. 6489/15).

A typical propaganda picture, of which the caption reads: 'Meeting at the front. The commander of a regiment at the western front has recognized one of his 'old comrades', who was with him in several scenes of war. The personal conversation only takes a few minutes, then both men return to their duties'. Pictures like these, with high ranking officers in personal meetings with ordinary soldiers, were often found.

The soldier has his shelter triangle over his shoulder and uses his worn-out K98k rifle to carry a batch of filled canteens. Western front, November 8, 1944.

(Museum of Modern History, Slovenia, No. 6116).

The original caption of this picture reads: '*Panzerfäuste*, still packed in crates, and only just received rifles for the newly deployed *Volkssturm* battalion are being unloaded from a truck'.

In many ways, this picture symbolizes the chaos of the last war months. Earlier in the war it would have been unthinkable to transport rifles in such a careless way, let alone that an officer would actually unload a truck. The men seem to empty the truck on a desolate country road, without any sign of the *Volkssturm* (People's army) battalion.

Moselle region, Western Germany, December 1944.

(Museum of Modern History, Slovenia, No. 6616/2).

'A messenger leaves a besieged position. The hole in the wall was created on purpose, since the front door of this building is located on the enemy side and every movement could be spotted by the Soviets', the German caption states. Even the propaganda department was not able anymore to produce an optimistic caption. This early production K98k, featuring a walnut stock, flat buttplate and hooded front sight, was probably produced in 1939. Until the moment this picture was taken, it had survived six years of warfare. Hungary, March 1945.
(Museum of Modern History, Slovenia, No. 6605/13).

# IX SOURCES, LITERATURE & NOTES

The information on which this book is based, stems from several sources. Apart from studying many weapons in official collections and thousands of original pictures, the most recent and elaborate literature was used. The most informative books on the K98k are those of Wacker and Law (two volumes): the first author is particularly strong in the field of the early history, accessories and use, while Law's major virtue is the detailed and extensive study of thousands of weapons, parts and markings.

Another major source is a collection of German documents, consisting of series of *Geheime Kommandosache. Überblick über den Rüstungsstand von Waffen'*, Wa J Rü (Wu G 2) (Survey of required and accepted amount of small arms), series of *Geheime Kommandosache. Fertigungsvorschau/Fertigungsbericht*, Wa J Rü (Wu G 2) (Manufacture/preview report) and the complete set of Mauser's *(Monats)Bericht der Waffenforschungsanstalt Oberndorf am Neckar* (Monthly report on the arms research department).

## Literature

- Ball, R.W.D., *Mauser Military Rifles of the World* (Iola 1996).
- Brandt, J.H., Hamann & Windisch, *Die Militärpatronen Kaliber 7,9 mm. Ihre Vorläufer und Abarten* (Schwäbisch Hall 1981).
- Eckardt, W. & O. Morawietz, *Die Handwaffen des brandenburgisch-preussisch-deutschen Heeres 1640-1945* (Hamburg 1973).
- Erbinger, M., *Schalldämpfer. Geschichte Technik Modelle* (Herne 1998).
- Götz, H.D., *German Military Rifles and Machine Pistols 1871-1945* (West Chester 1990).
- Haas, F. de, *Bolt Action Rifles* (Northbrook 1995,3).
- Hahn, F., *Weapons and Secret Weapons of the German Army, 1933-1945* (Koblenz 1987).
- Handrich, H.D., *Vom Gewehr 98 zum Sturmgewehr* (Herford 1993).
- Kent, D.W., *German 7.92 mm Military Ammunition 1888-1945* (Ann Arbor 1973).
- Law, R.D., *Backbone of the Wehrmacht. The German K98k Rifle 1934-1945* (Ontario 1993).
- Law, R.D., *Sniper Variations of the German K98k Rifle* (Ontario 1996).
- Lehner, H., 'Die ersten deutschen Militärkarabiner 98', *Deutsches Waffen Journal*, 5/1984, 568-572; 6/1984, 738-742; 7/1984, 874-877.
- Oberkommando des Heeres, *Liste der Fertigungskennzeichen für Waffen, Munition und Gerät* (Berlin 1944).
- Olson, L., 'Identifying Mauser Markings', *The American Rifleman* 87, January 1971, 86-91.
- Olson, L., *Mauser Bolt Rifles* (Montezuma 1976,3).
- Pawlas, K. *Waffenrevue* 'Der Karabiner 98 kurz' Vol. 1, 1971, 81- ; 'Das Gewehrgranatgerät (Schiessbecher)', Vol. 3, 1971, 443-470 & Vol. 4,1972, 605-612; 'Zielfernrohrkarabiner 98k' Vol. 5, 1972, 783-788;'Gewehr-granatgerät' Vol. 12, 1974, 1851-1856; 'Einsteckläufe für Schusswaffen 98' Vol. 32, 1979, 5049-5056; 'System 98 für Fallschirmjäger', Vol. 46, 1982, 7291-7300; 'Scharfschützen-Sonderausstattung: Spiegelkolben, Grabenspiegel, Deckungszielgerät', Vol. 48, 1983, 7595-7616.
- Schmid, H.P., 'Der Not gehorchend. Die Endkriegsproduktion des Karabiners 98k und VK98', *Deutsches*

*Waffen Journal* 34, 9, September 1998, 1408-1415.

- Schmid, W., 'In letzter Sekunde. Noch ein 98er..!', *Deutsches Waffen Journal* 35, 6, June 1999, 876-879.

- Senich, P., *The German Sniper 1941-1945* (Boulder 1982).

- Speed, J., W. Schmid & R. Herrmann, *Original Oberndorf Sporting Rifles* (Ontario 1997).

- Speed, J., *Mauser Smallbores Sporting, Target & Training Rifles* (Ontario 1998).

- Wacker, A., *Das System Adalbert. Der K98k* (Düsseldorf 1993).

**Notes**

1) The best information on the early development of 'system 98' carbines is to be found in the H. Lehner's three volume series in the *Deutsches Waffen Journal*.

2) H.D. Handrich,, *Vom Gewehr 98 zum Sturmgewehr* (Herford 1993), 27.

3) A. Wacker, *Das System Adalbert. Der K98k* (Düsseldorf 1993), 7.

4) Handrich, 27

5) R.D. Law, *Backbone of the Wehrmacht. The German K98k Rifle 1934-1945* (Ontario 1993), 5-11.

6) W. Schmid, 'In letzter Sekunde. Noch ein 98er..!', *Deutsches Waffen Journal* 35, 6, June 1999, 876-879.

7) Wacker, 31.

8) The best information on German sniper training, camouflage etc. is to be found in P. Senich's, *The German Sniper 1941-1945* (Boulder 1982).

9) For a far more detailed description of all variants and sub-variants, see: Law, R.D., *Sniper Variations of the German K98k Rifle* (Ontario 1996).

10) These figures stem from the *Geheime Kommandosache. Überblick über den Rüstungsstand von Waffen'*, *Wa J Rü (Wu G 2)* and *Geheime Kommandosache Fertigungsvorschau/Fertigungsbericht, Wa J Rü (Wu G 2)*

11) For a complete description of all variants, see: J. Speed, *Mauser Smallbores Sporting, Target & Training Rifles* (Ontario 1998).

13) For a detailed technical description of the K98k system, see: F. de Haas, *Bolt Action Rifles* (Northbrook 1995,3).

14) M. Erbinger, M., *Schalldämpfer. Geschichte Technik Modelle* (Herne 1998), 72.

15) For detailed information on the German 7.9 mm cartridge, see: J.H. Brandt, H.H. Hamann & Windisch, *Die Militärpatronen Kaliber 7,9 mm. IhreVorläufer und Abarten* (Schwäbisch Hall 1981) and D.W. Kent, *German 7.92 mm Military Ammunition 1888-1945* (Ann Arbor 1973).